the E

WISDOM FOR LIFE

Volume 1

*A 90 - day inspirational devotional
guide for your daily living*

Thanks for your support toward
the success of 18th Encounter
Retreat. May God richly bless
and reward your labour for
His Kingdom.

Bunde & Bose
the Encounter Int'l
Calgary, Canada
March 2018

'Bode Akindele

©2014 'Bode Akindele

ISBN: 978-1-304-64646-0

The Incubator International
P. O. Box 680
St. Paul, Alberta, Canada
T0A 3A0
Tel: +17806457722

E. Mail: bode@theincubatorintl.org

Website: www.theincubatorintl.org

Bible quotes are from the King James Version unless otherwise
stated.

Dedication

I want to dedicate this volume to:
Tomi, **Titobi**, **Timileyin** and **Tunmise**;
Our four children who have agreed to embrace the habit of daily devotion in the word and prayer.

Acknowledgement

I am grateful to God for giving me the opportunity to come across the truth contained in this devotional. I am glad for the insight, and for leading every step of the way up to the point of coming up with packaging the messages in this format.

I appreciate the faith and encouragement of my first radio producer, Danny White (Wiebe) who embraced my broadcast idea until we experienced the breakthrough.

I must appreciate my daughters; Tomi and Titobi, who agreed to help me at the start with the laborious work of transcription of the audio messages. I thank Ileri Oyedele for spending most of his summer break working with me on this project. My nephew Oluwaseyitanfunwa Oke did an amazing job on the cover design. The motivation and assistance of Rev. and Pastor (Mrs.) Olowosoyo during the publishing process is invaluable and much appreciated. I want to say a big thank you to all those that sent me positive feedback on the audio version of the daily devotionals. Most importantly I want to thank and appreciate my love and 'pie', Olukemi, for all her continual support, assistance and encouragement.

Introduction

I was invited some years ago to speak at the birthday celebration of my friend. As I prepared for the event, the Holy Spirit directed me to the book of Proverbs. I decided to exhort on 'the wise woman', and 'the virtuous woman'. After that event, I decided to study the entire book of Proverbs again. God opened my eyes in a new way and I noticed that virtually every issue of life is addressed in this inspirational book. Coupled with other portions of the scriptures, I found again that the wisdom needed to navigate every aspect of life is in the bible. This began my long journey into the book of Proverbs – I am yet to get to the final stop!

I must thank Dr. & Mrs. Yinka Dada for the invitation to that party – that is the genesis.

Not long after my study began, I started a daily 3 minutes radio broadcast on our local community radio. Then the audience grew through the internet. The feedback I received indicated that listeners were able to apply the principles highlighted to their everyday life. This first volume of 'Wisdom for Life' is a part of the messages. I am certain you will find answers to diverse questions of life.

Proverbs 4:20 (NLT) says;

'My son, pay attention to what I say. Listen carefully to my words. Don't lose sight of them. Let them penetrate deep into your heart, for they bring life to those who find them, and healing to their whole body.'

Read through each day's devotional and meditate on the scriptural references to gain your own personal revelation. Read it again and again if you need to, and share it with someone else. It will bless you.

Contents

Day 1   Begin with God

*'In the beginning God created the heavens and the
earth'*   *Gen 1:1*

At the beginning of all things, we see God. He is the origin and
the creator of all things. All things found their start in Him.
The scripture says all things hold together in Christ (Col 1:17).
At the beginning of every phase of our lives, it is an
opportunity to establish God at the helms of our affairs, and
commit all things to His hands afresh. It has become a tradition
for people at the beginning of a new year to make new
resolutions and new plans, purchase new clothes, prepare
special delicacies and of course have special gatherings.

At this time, I would want to encourage you to review your
past year and put the new in clear perspective. Today gives you
an opportunity to rekindle your hopes of achieving your God
given dreams and aspirations. You can 'begin life again' as it
were. Take advantage of this day. Make today your fresh
beginning. Decide to give God priority in every affairs of your
life. Decide to approach your life with fresh hope and vigour.
Decide to go for the best that God has for you in faith. Decide
today to live your life pleasing to the Lord.

Take your relationship, business or career to the next level with
God. Commit your ways afresh to the Lord and make up your
mind to follow His views, instructions and guidance every day
of this New Year. Acknowledge Him and He will surely direct
your path and perfect all that concerns you. Do have a peaceful
and fruitful New Year, in Jesus name.

Day 2   The Principal Thing

'Wisdom is the principal thing; therefore get wisdom: and with all your getting, get understanding'   *Proverbs 4:7*

After you have committed your way to the Lord in the New Year; you need the wisdom to navigate your way through the entire year. Our scripture today makes it clear that your principal pursuit should be for wisdom, and I believe it is available otherwise God would not say we should 'get it'.

Eccl 10:15 says *'The labour of the foolish wearieth every one of them; because he knoweth not how to go to the city'*. The foolish labour quite all right, but it leads not only to his frustration, but everybody with him is wearied! Wisdom gives you 'the how' to do all that you have to do, in order to see your prayers come to pass through the year. That wisdom is available as you seek God in prayer and as you look daily in His word. Make that your pursuit this year; determine to daily seek God and meditate on His word. Do this and you will daily find the light and direction to your path of success.

Remember this: God has all the wisdom you need to handle every issue that you will be faced with this year. Determine to seek God and His word daily to get the wisdom you need. Start today.

Day 3   The Beginning of Wisdom

> 'The fear of the Lord is the beginning of knowledge: but fools despise wisdom and instruction'
>   Proverbs 4:7

The message version says 'start with God – the first step in learning is bowing down to God; only fools thumb their noses at such wisdom and learning'. The truth is this; the more of God you know and the more you imbibe God's ways, the more wisdom in dealing with all life's issues you possess.

Job 28:20 – 28 in Message version is a very interesting read…

"So, where does Wisdom come from? And where does Insight live? It can't be found by looking, no matter how deep you dig, no matter how high you fly. If you search through the graveyard and question the dead, they say, 'we've only heard rumors of it.' God alone knows the way to Wisdom; he knows the exact place to find it. He knows where everything is on earth, he sees everything under heaven. After he commanded the winds to blow and measured out the waters, arranged for the rain and set off explosions of thunder and lightning, He focused on Wisdom, made sure it was all set and tested and ready. Then he addressed the human race: 'Here it is! Fear-of-the-Lord-that's Wisdom and Insight means shunning evil.'"

The fear of the Lord here means the reverence for God, based on your knowledge of Him. Determine to walk in reverence for God as regards every aspect of your life today and you will discover that you will find it easy to know the right thing to do each time; you certainly will walk in all-round wisdom.

Day 4 By Humility and the Fear of the Lord

*"By humility and the fear of the Lord are riches,
and honour, and life" Proverbs 22:4*

Everyone desires a satisfying life, marked with riches and
honour. My prayer is that this year will be such for you, in
Jesus name. The question is; 'how do we get that kind of life?'
Today's scripture gives us the answer – by humility and the
fear of the Lord. So, determine to cooperate with God so that
this year will be characterised by riches, honour and complete
satisfaction.

Humility is generally defined in the dictionary as 'the quality
of not thinking that you are better than other people'. So,
humility is in the heart and nobody may 'see' it ordinarily. In
the contest of this scripture, it more so refers to your
relationship with God. Simply put, 'you do not think your idea
is better than that of God's'! Maintain a humble attitude toward
every man and more importantly, toward God. No matter what
you think about anything, God's view wins – God's word is
final!

Maintain this attitude at home, at work, in church, and in the
community. In addition to this, walk daily in reverential fear of
God. You will be amazed how you will walk into riches, great
honour before God and man, as well as a fulfilling long life.

Day 5 Understanding the Fear of the Lord

> *'My son, if thou wilt receive my words, and hide my commandments with thee; ...Then shalt thou understand the fear of the Lord, and find the knowledge of God' Proverbs 2:1-5*

The scripture makes it clear to us that 'the fear of the Lord is the beginning of wisdom' (Pr. 1:7). Many times the concept of 'the fear of the Lord' sounds mysterious and scary. In today's scripture, the Lord has laid it plain to us how to walk in reverential fear of God.

1. Receive God's word, and hide it in your heart (verse 1). Do this daily and deliberately. You will know God's opinion about every life issue.
2. Determine to make God's word the basis of your opinion and decisions on every life issue.

When you do this, you will be able to give heed to, or pay attention to God's wisdom for your daily life. Verses 3 & 4 of proverbs 2 states clearly that we should place emphases on the both study and obeying God's word. This seems to me that we cannot be flimsy when it comes to reading and studying and living by the word.

When you give daily attention to the study of God's word (not so much about volume, but about consistency and adequate proportion), and put it into practice, you will naturally get to know God, and you will find it normal to walk in reverential fear of Him. The result is that your way will be marked with riches, honour and good life (Proverbs 22:4).

Day 6   Years of a life worth living

> *"My son, forget not my law or teaching, but let your heart keep my commandments; for length of days and years of a life (worth living) and tranquillity (inward and outward and continuing through old age till death), these shall they add to you". Proverbs 3:1-2 Amp*

I would like us to meditate on these two verses of scriptures. It gives a very simple but precise key to a good life! I like the contemporary English version; *'My child, remember my teachings and instructions and obey them completely. They will help you live a long and prosperous life'.*

The key here is to completely obey God's teachings and instructions. The word of God addresses every issue of life; your health, marriage, business, etc. If you would take these instructions to heart and obey them, you will enjoy your every day on this earth.

My prayer is that you will live a long, strong, and fulfilled life in Jesus name, amen. Have a great day.

Other scriptures: Deut. 28:1-14

Day 7   Trust in the Lord

> *'Trust in the Lord with all your heart, and lean not on your own understanding; in all your ways acknowledge Him, And He shall direct your paths. Do not be wise in your own eyes; Fear the Lord and depart from evil. It will be health to your flesh, and strength to your bones'. Proverbs 3:5-8 NKJV*

At the beginning of a new year, new job or a new phase of life; say a fresh marriage relationship, for example; we are filled with fresh hopes. New beginning presents fresh opportunities & aspirations. On the other hand, they are also characterised with the concerns of the unknown. As you begin this New Year, our scripture for today is well spelt out in the Contemporary English version:

With your heart you must trust the Lord and not your judgement. Always let him lead you, and he will clear the road for you to follow. Don't ever think that you are wise enough, but respect the Lord and stay away from evil. This will make you healthy, and you will feel strong'

Do not depend on your past experiences. No matter what you see, feel, think, or hear. Determine to trust God and allow him lead you. You are set for a peaceful and prosperous year, in Jesus name.

Day 8   Your Storage Places will be Filled-up

> *'Honour the Lord with your possessions, And with the first fruits of all your increase; so your bans will be filled with plenty, and our vast will overflow with new wine'. Proverbs 3:9-10 NKJV*

This scripture states clearly the way to have abundance. I like the message version: 'Honour God with everything you own; give him the first and the best. Your barns will burst; your wine vast will brim over'. You now have in your hands the blueprint for the path to increase and great wealth. This is the lifestyle of the kingdom of God. It is God's way of doing things with regards to wealth creation and sustenance.

Gen 8:22 says *'while the earth remains, seed time and harvest ... shall not cease'*. The way to have is to give. This is a number one principle of the kingdom. This principle actually applies to every aspect of life. You need a friend, be friendly; you want to be loved, give love; you desire to be respected more, give respect; etc. So, for you to enjoy God's abundance this year, make up your mind to live a lifestyle of giving. Faithfully pay your tithe and give offerings, and your barns will be filled with plenty and your cruse of oil will never run dry. Think through and make sure you Start NOW.

Day 9   Sell Everything and Buy Wisdom

'Above all and before all, do this: get wisdom! Write this at the top of your list: Get understanding. Throw your arms around her – believe me, you won't regret it, Never let her go – she'll make your life glorious. She'll garland your life with grace, she'll festoon your days with beauty'. Proverbs 4:7-9 MSG

The King James Version of today's scripture starts by saying *'wisdom is the principal thing; therefore get wisdom'*. Make it your priority to obtain the mind of God concerning everything before you act. If you would soak your heart and mind with the way God thinks about every issue of life, you will have the mind of God and will be able to build your life on wisdom. Your life will be made glorious and certainly you will be very glad with the result.

The entire world was formed by God's wisdom (Ps 104:24).

Take time to think through on your ideas and the different decisions you need to make. Base your thoughts on the principles of the word. Give all it takes to get God's mind before you act. This was what Solomon's father told him when he was young;

'When I was a boy at my father's knee, the pride and joy of my mother, He would sit me down and drill me: 'Take this to heart. Do what I tell you – live! Sell everything and buy wisdom! Forage for understanding! Don't forget one word! Don't deviate an inch! Proverbs 4:3-5 MSG

Day 10   Essential foundation layers

> *"It takes wisdom to build a house, and understanding to set it on a firm foundation: it takes knowledge to furnish the rooms with fine furniture and beautiful draperies. It is better to be wise than strong; intelligence outranks muscle any day. Strategic planning is the key to warfare; to win, you need a lot of good counsel". Proverbs 24:3-6 MSG*

Wisdom, understanding and knowledge are three essential layers of the foundation for anything you do or want to become. Your home can only come out well built if it is founded on this composite foundation.

I believe wisdom is simply 'the ability to access the mind of God' about any matter. Understanding is an act of wisdom. These two 'attributes' can only be seen in manifestation, though you might not be able to touch them. We know when the wind is blowing because of its effects that we see! Your depth of knowledge depends on the information you can gather around you. It is by your level of knowledge that you can bring heavenly insight (which is a combination of wisdom and understanding) to benefit the human race in this terrestrial world.

Wisdom begins as you deliberately seek to access divine information. Start by seeking God's mind about your home or business. Then equip yourself with information around you, in light of what heaven has revealed to you. Read wide, ask questions, and seek counsel if necessary. Then you can effect what you 'saw' and do it beautifully. It's not too late to lay this essential foundation. Remember, strategic planning is the key to warfare. This year will be your year of winning.

Day 11   Build in Proper Order – 1st Things 1st

"First plant your fields; then build your barn"
Proverbs 24:27

This is wisdom. Do the 1st things 1st. Let your priorities be right. A farmer will only need the barn to keep the harvest. He will have crop to harvest only if he had planted! Get a clear plan before you begin to build. Take care of your own home before you can have strength to care for others. This is the principle we see here; and it is good to apply it at this early part of the year.

So, take time to think about your life. For example, it might be wise for you to sit for one more professional exam and pass it before you apply for the next position. Sow your bountiful seed, and then expect the plentiful harvest. There is a time in life that you work hard and invest; later in life you expect dividends. Notice the word 'fields'; plant your fields. Ask God to show you the different aspects that you can invest in, and then take the necessary action. When it is harvest time, your barn will certainly be full to overflow.

Amplified version puts the verse this way: '[Put first things first.] Prepare your work outside and get it ready for yourself in the field; and afterwards build your house and establish a home.' I believe this is some dimension of wisdom for single people to consider when planning for their future.

May you walk in divine wisdom in every aspect of your life this year, in Jesus name; have a great day.

Day 12   "…And Don't be Lazy"

"One day I walked by the field of an old lazybones, and then passed the vineyard of a lout; they were overgrown with weeds, thick with thistles, all the fences broken down. I took a long look and pondered what I saw; the fields preached me a sermon and I listened: 'A nap here, a nap there, a day off here, a day off there, sit back take it easy – do you know what come next? Just this: You can look forward to dirt-poor life, with poverty as your permanent houseguest!" Proverbs 24:30 – 34 MSG

A lazy man does not have understanding. Whatever ideas you might have; however great a potential you possess; without diligent hard work, it cannot come to fruition. However great a plan you might have received of the Lord and properly written out, if you do not arise and diligently execute them, there can be no beauty and prosperity.

You might succeed to plant a vast field of grain and you built a barn of stones, all well laid out; without a lifestyle of sustained disciplined and diligence, everything will waste away with time.

Diligence is simply 'you consistently daily working on your field.' Do not procrastinate, do not be slack. Work at the time of work and sleep at the time of sleep. This is wisdom. Otherwise, it would 'suddenly' dawn on you that you have wasted your opportunity and you have become a permanent host of poverty, ensnared by its nuisance. Please do not be lazy. Take time to think right now and make necessary adjustments in your lifestyle.

Day 13 '...Feeble but Wise...'

> *"There are four things which are little on the earth, but they are exceedingly wise: The ants are a people not strong, yet they prepare their food in the summer. The rock badgers are a feeble folk, yet they make their homes in the crags. The locusts have no king, yet they are all advance in ranks. The spider skilfully grasps with its hands, and it is in kings' palaces" Proverbs 30:24-28 NKJV*

If you could spend some time to study these four verses of scripture in as many translations as you can lay your hands upon, including probably the Bible in your local language; you will come to understand that your circumstances are not enough to limit your achievements and rising in life.

Imagine how frail the ants are, yet they succeed in storing up in summer all the food they will need in winter; I wonder at their wisdom (Proverbs 6:6-8). The conies seem to be weak, yet they make their homes among the rocks! Locusts have no king, yet they go forward in formation – I wonder how they do that! Also, lizards and spiders which you can easily hold in your hands sneaks past vigilant royal guards to dwell in palaces! God has given each of these four small creatures the wisdom and inherent abilities to survive in different life situations despite how feeble they are; the wonderworks of God!

If you would look inward, and lift your heart unto God for wisdom, you will receive the light you need to come out of every predicament of life. *'...Fear not therefore: you are of more value than many sparrows (Luke 12:7).'* This year is a fresh opportunity from God to you; take it with wisdom.

Day 14   Be Diligent

'He who has a slack hand becomes poor, but the hand of the diligent makes rich' Pr. 10:4 NKJV

The question to ask from ourselves today is this: Do you want to be rich? Then be diligent. If you deal with a slack hand, the Bible says you will become poor.

The lesson here is '...don't envy a wealthy man if you are a lazy person.' If you have a job right now, work diligently as if you are the owner of the company. The owner will be happy for your work attitude and in response, you will be promoted – isn't that a win-win situation? The Bible says *'...he that gathers in summer is a wise son... (verse 5);'* so do your work on-time and do not delay assignments. As you go to work today, determine that you will not procrastinate on any assignment you are given. If you are fond of procrastinating, you have to pray that God will help you overcome this lifestyle while you determine to make necessary changes.

We can make the following conclusions from our study today: He that wants to be poor would work like a lazy person, but he that wants to be rich should work diligently. May God bless and prosper your ways today, in Jesus name.

Day 15   Maximize Your Potential

'He that tilleth his land shall be satisfied with bread: but he that followeth vain persons is void of understanding'. Proverbs 12:11

You would notice the following points from today's scripture:

It is a different thing to have a land and to till the land; it is a different thing to be gifted and to work hard at your gifting. It is one thing to have a job and it is another thing to work your job. It is something to have an idea and it is another to maximize the thoughts that God has given to you.

Look at that scripture again: *'he that tilleth his land shall be satisfied with bread'*. So, it is only the person that works on his gifting that will have bread. Anywhere in the Bible you find the word bread; it talks of wealth, money, abundance, etc. So, if you don't work hard on the gifting, the opportunities or the provisions that God has given to you, you won't have wealth.

Do you want to be wealthy? Till your ground! Go to school and study, go to work and work hard at your job. Let the ideas in your head be put on paper; then be stimulated to work on them. When the results come, it will turn to bread for you and for as many as are aquatinted with you. Don't fool around at your workplace today, work; and as you do so, the Lord will prosper you and make your day fruitful. This is wisdom for life.

Day 16 How Long Will You Sleep?

'How long will you lie there doing nothing at all?
When are you going to get up and stop sleeping?
Sleep a little. Doze a little. Fold your hands and
twiddle your thumbs. Suddenly, everything is gone,
as though it had been taken by an armed robber.'
Proverbs 6:9-11 CEV

When lack pursues a man that does not have, it does so like an armed robber, very violent! When a man that does not have realises his state of lack, he becomes frustrated. Often times, too much sleep leads to poverty. Don't let too much sleep hinder you from tilling your ground and from maximizing your potential. For how long would you sleep?

Wake up to your responsibilities. You need to wake up from your slumber and think through on the dreams that God has given to you. You have told many people that you have ideas, but nobody can see it effected, you need to wake up to implement your ideas. For how long would you remain in the state of stupor? Wake up. If you sleep for too long; it will lead you to poverty. If you lie down doing nothing, you are indirectly sleeping!

Poverty brings a sense of regrets, and this can lead to a frustrated destiny. Do not delay any further. Right now, take some time to think through on all the ideas that God has given you before, write them down, and review the ones you wrote before. Determine the plan of action for the implementation, trust the Lord to lead you, follow Him in faith, and mountain will melt before you like wax before fire. This is your day of fresh grace. May God give you wisdom and understanding!

Day 17   Hand of diligence bear rule

Work hard, and you will be a leader; be lazy, and
you will end up a slave. (CEV)
The slothful man does catch his game or roast it
once he kills it, but the diligent man gets precious
possessions. (Amp) Proverbs 12: 24 & 27

If we can imbibe what the Bible teaches regarding a life style
of diligence each family will prosper, the community will
prosper and the nation will be built up.

You will find that the heaven is so wide; the birds don't
collide! Many times when you find a man that complains that
he is not in leadership, it could be because he has misused the
opportunities he once had. But since you are still alive today,
there is still another opportunity for you to build a future for
yourself and fulfil your destiny. One way to do that is to be
diligent in what you do. A man that is diligent, it does not
matter what he does, will rise to the top.

The Bible says *'he will stand before kings, not before mean*
men'. Consider verse 27 again, imagine a slothful man; he goes
to hunting but is too lazy to roast what he brought home! He
seem to make some attempts, but he has not the consistency
and determination to see it through! Are you like that, with the
many opportunities at your disposal? Why would you be so
lazy and loose the opportunities to do great things for yourself,
your family and the community? Wake up! The substance of a
diligent man is precious. May God bless you as you renew
your commitment to walking in diligence today.

Day 18   Labour in Truthfulness

'Wealth gotten by vanity shall be diminished: but he that gathereth by labour shall increase.'
Proverbs 13:11

We've been studying about diligence as an attitude and lifestyle. You need to work hard with clear principles. Some people work hard in deceit, while others work and labour hard in truthfulness. You need to work hard with clear a principle of truthfulness.

'He that gathers by labour shall increase.' No matter what you do, one thing is certain, if you are working consistently hard at your job, you are bound to increase. However, if anyone is doing business with deceit, he might increase for now, but the Bible says it will diminish.

So, while we emphasize diligent attitude, make sure that you balance it with a right frame of mind that your labour must be based on truthfulness. You can be rest assured that when you gather wealth by truthfulness and hard work, it leads to sustainable increase. If your truthful hard work today does not seem to amount to much, do not worry. A little addition each day will eventually add up. Don't be in a hurry to amass wealth unjustly overnight. Otherwise it will diminish. What will certainly increase is the wealth that you gather by truthful labour.

Don't be ashamed to work hard at what you are doing; just be consistent in your hard work. The little increase of each day will add up, and tomorrow you will be the happier for it. This is our decision today; labour consistently in truthfulness and you will be sustained in wealth. God bless your day.

Day 19   Don't be a Waster

'He also that is slothful in his work is brother to him that is a great waster' Proverbs 18:9

Many people have lost opportunities before and they regret it. But instead of regret, we only need to make a decision to change and never waste opportunities again – do not live in the regret and loss. However, slothfulness or laziness will lead to a wasted opportunity; time lost can never be regained.

So whether you are self-employed or an employee in a company, make up your mind not to be slothful. As a matter of fact, any employer should not keep a lazy person at work, because they are actually great wasters! If you have ideas, or thoughts, or great capacity and you are slothful, then you are wasting God's resources.

The way you maximize the little opportunity God has presented to you where you are is what matters. This is our decision today; I will bend down and work on the ideas and opportunities available to me and will not be lazy. Otherwise you will equal someone who is wasting divine resources. May God prosper you in all you do, in Jesus name.

Day 20   Seize the Opportunity

'A man's gift makes room for him, and brings him before great men'. Proverbs 18:16 NKJV

Make the most of the opportunity coming your way today; it will lead you to your promotion. Determine that you will work hard on your gifts. It is when your gifting is tapped to the maximum that you will experience elevation and publicity where it matters.

You might have gifts, but when the opportunity comes for you to exercise your gifting and you are lazy, it is a disadvantage. So, be on the watch, seize your opportunity when presents itself.

It is when people observe how good you are at what you do that the promotion will come. It is when they see your consistent hard work that the opportunity for consideration for promotion will come. Lifting does not drop on someone's laps without them going out there and doing something.

It is from the observation of the little you currently do, that the potential of your greatness will be seen; then you will continue to grow. *'He who is faithful in little, is already judged faithful in much'! (Luke 16:10)* This is the wisdom today; make the most of the opportunity in front of you today, it will lead to your greater tomorrow. May God bless you and grant you great success as you face your day, in Jesus name, amen.

Day 21   Don't give Excuses

'The sluggard will not plough by reason of the cold
therefore shall he beg in harvest and have nothing'
Proverbs 20:4

When it is cold, it is naturally understandable for a farmer to keep indoors; however the Bible says here that anybody who does not plough because of the cold is a lazy person. I think what God is saying is 'don't give excuses for your laziness based on even obvious reasons'.

When you are someone that always finds excuses to give for your inability to accomplish a task, it may look legitimate, but a day will come when your boss will be willing to be understanding with you no more.

You have to make up your mind, no matter what the weather or the situation is like, that you will brace up and do what is expected of you. Determine that in-spite of the obstacles, you will forge ahead. The working environment might not be friendly or conducive; do not look for excuses, but be determined that despite the challenges, you will arise and achieve what is expected of you. As you do this, you will prosper in all your life's pursuits.

Day 22   Your Labour Leads to Plenty

The thoughts of the diligent tend only to plenteousness; but of every one that is hasty only to want....' The desire of the slothful killeth him; for his hands refuse to labour'. Proverbs 21: 5, 25

The desire of the slothful kills him because his hands refuse to labor! You might have two people, both with desires and good ideas, very genuine proposals; the two of them might end up at different points. Imagine that one of them invests time to diligently implement his/her ideas or thoughts while the other does not.

The Bible says the result for the one that implements the ideas will only be plenteousness! As long as you put efforts into your thoughts, desire and ideas, you are destined for the path of plenteous increase, and prosperity. To the one that refuses to labour at the desires and ideas, it is that desire that will kill him because the resulting frustration will lead him to do evil things – he will worry, stress and at the end will not prosper!

I like the Good News Version: *"⁵If you plan and work hard, you will have plenty; if you hurry to get rich, you will end up poor. ²⁵If you want too much and are too lazy to work, it could be fatal."* You might have grandeur plans; but if you are too lazy to back it up with hard work, you will end up poor; and that could be fatal! Get your ideas; work at them, and you will prosper, in Jesus name.

Day 23   Be Healed of Your Past; Be Established in Your Today

> *"And Joseph called the name of the first born Manasseh: For God, said he, hath made me forget all my toil, and all my father's house. And the name of the second called he Ephraim: for God caused me to be fruitful in the land of my affliction"*
> *Genesis 41:51-52*

Thinking about the sequence of the names Joseph gave his sons, it occurred to my mind that the sequence is significant. His first son was named Manasseh - 'for God has made me forget all my toil and my entire father's house'. Obviously until this time, his mind was occupied with the loss of his father's love, the hatred of his brothers, his time in the pit, the unjust accusation and report of Potiphar's wife and the consequent jail term! God helped him to forget those days by the arrival of this son. He named his second son Ephraim - 'for God has caused me to be fruitful in the land of my affliction'.

Everyone need to first get to 'the point of Manasseh' before he can get to 'the state of Ephraim'. Until you forget the past you cannot get to your future! When Jacob (Israel) was blessing the boys later (Gen. 48:17-19), he set Ephraim before Manasseh! Ephraim stands for your future, and I can say to you now that; 'what God still have in store for you is more glorious than whatever you might have experienced in your past'. Determine to let go of the pains of the past. Forgive those that offended and ill-treated you. Forgive yourself, forgive your past. Embrace today with hope as you walk towards your future. More so, remember that today is the future you were hoping for, receive it with faith.

Day 24   You need to spend time with God

'Through desire a man, having separated himself seeketh and intermeddleth with all wisdom'
Proverbs 18:1

Your success in life is not determined by how much labour you exert on your activities; but it is first determined by the amount of time you spend with God on a regular basis. You need to separate yourself from time to time, and seek the God of all wisdom. The scripture says 'you will intermingle with all wisdom'. Notice that it takes personal desire; you have to purposely set that appointment with God and keep it.

This exercise goes beyond the short time you spend to have your required daily 'quiet time' of devotion. This is the time you think through and weigh all life questions with the principles of God's word. It is the time set aside for prayerful meditative thinking with your regenerated mind! You ask God questions and you listen for His answers.

Daniel and his team were confronted with death because King Nebuchadnezzar had a frightening dream he could not remember (Daniel chapter 2). Daniel went in and desired of the king that he would give him time, and that he would show the king the interpretation (v16). The secret which astrologers, magicians and soothsayers could not access was revealed to Daniel. You will receive answers to all life threatening questions as you spend time with *'the God in heaven that revealeth secrets' (v28)*. You will obtain all the wisdom you need for a fruitful, meaningful and peaceful life, as you invest time with the God of all wisdom. Forever may the Lord bless you, in Jesus name, amen.

Day 25   Counsel = Water in Deep Well

'A person's thoughts are like water in deep well but someone with insight can draw them out' Proverbs 20:5 GNB

Diligence at work is more than working harder, it involves working smarter. Diligently thinking through on different issues will lead to smart working. It takes someone with insight to draw out counsel from great depths to the surface. Consider 'water in a deep well' – it is not contaminated but pure; however it takes time to get to it.

Take your time and reach to attain counsel through your regenerated mind; do not rush, always allow adequate time to think through. There is treasure in your regenerated mind!

It takes deep thoughts to search out the mind of God on issues of life (be it marriage, carrier or ministry). When you successfully think through, light will come to you and you will be able to take your next flight. Then gentiles will come to your light and kings to your rising (Isaiah 60:1-3).

Day 26   Leaders Think Broad, Deep and Wide

> '...It is the glory of God to conceal a thing; but the
> honor of kings is to search out a matter. The heaven
> for height, and the earth for depth, and the heart of
> kings is unsearchable' Proverbs 25:1-3

Verse 1 indicated that these are some of the proverbs of
Solomon copied out by the men of King Hezekiah of Judah.
Every leader needs to give attention to them. 1Kings 4:34 says
*'And there came of all people to hear the Wisdom of Solomon,
from all kings of the earth, which had heard of his wisdom'*.
Leaders are keen to spend adequate time to search out the mind
of God on various matters. It is the honour of kings to search
out a matter.

Think through as you meditate on God's word to search out
secrete things of God on each subject. Ps 119:18 says there are
wondrous things in the word of God. Be a king as you develop
the habit of thinking through in your closet, to search out
God's mind on different issues before you act. The saying goes
'great leaders are great thinkers'.

Consider the message version of verse 3. *'Like the horizon for
breath and the oceans for depth the understanding of a leader
is broad and deep'*. For you to be successful in leadership and
in business, you need to invest time before God in thinking
through. You will receive light concerning dark difficult
things; and when you come out from your thinking corner, you
will act appropriately. Then you will not have any reason to
worry!

Other Scriptures: Ps 92:5;

Day 27   Coordinate Your Thoughts Well

> *'An idea well expressed is like a design of Gold set in Silver' Proverbs 25:11 GNB*
> *'A word fitly spoken is like apples of gold in pictures of silver' Proverbs 25:11*

For you to get to the point where your ideas are well coordinated, you must have thought about them over and over again. The business idea that God gives you must not be rushed into the market place; you need to think through them until you arrive at a way of expression; so fitting that it is like apples of gold in pictures of silver.

Analyse the ideas well enough until you can present it with an advantage. Don't waste your God given ideas because you rushed out from your thinking closet too early; invest adequate time to think. You might need to do some indebt facts finding around the matter. Carry out some SWOT (strength, weakness, opportunity and threat) analysis and this will guide you on how to approach the implementation of those divine ideas.

Pr. 20:18 says *'every purpose is established by counsel: and with good advice make war'*. Remember, you have access to divine insight that the world does not have! So, in these uncertain times, you can still take steps with certainty and fly with clarity. You will know when, how, and where to launch your ideas. Plus, you will receive strategic ideas on who should be present at your first presentation! The message version of Pr. 25:11 says *'The right word at the right time is like a custom made piece of jewellery'*.

Day 28   A Portion of God's Wisdom

'O Lord, how manifold are thy works! In wisdom
hart though made them all; the earth is full of thy
riches'. Psalm 104:24

I like the Contemporary English Version of this scripture; *'Our*
Lord, by your wisdom you made so many things ...' God wants
to give you a portion of the wisdom by which He has made all
things. As you spend time with Him daily, reach out for the
divine wisdom from God on all life's issues. Reach Out for it.
Make the most of your time in God's presence. God actually
instructs us to make a demand on Him for this! Look at
Contemporary English version of James 1:5; *'If any of you*
need wisdom, you should ask God, and it will be given to you.
God is generous and won't correct you for asking'. This is a
special invitation with and an open cheque to ask for as much
and however varied wisdom we need. God is waiting on you to
ask, He wants to help you through everything in life.

Ps 104:24 concludes by saying, *'... the earth is full of your*
riches'. When you access divine wisdom, you will access a
portion of the riches that fills the earth. This is the truth. Eccl
5:9 says; *'... the profit of the earth is for all: the king himself is*
served by the field'. You have equal right to earth's riches.

You will access the riches that the earth offers if you will daily
invest time to access wisdom from the maker of heaven and the
earth. Deliberately spend some time today and REACH OUT
for heavens wisdom as you meditatively think-through.

Day 29   Clarity of Thought

> *'The thought of the diligent tend only to plenteousness; but of every one that is hasty only to want' Proverbs 21:5*

If you want to be successful in life, you need to be clear of what you are up to. Many people are in too much of a hurry to become rich or to succeed, but do not have a clear goal. Clarity is very vital in leadership, in communication, in business, in relationship and in life generally.

On the one hand, it is good to work diligently, but hard work without first diligently thinking through leads to frustration. There is a popular phrase; 'Quo Vadis', 'where are you going'? Is your vision clear, do you have clarity of purpose about the subject in hand? If you know where you are going, you will be focused on what you need to do, while you avoid irrelevancies.

Anyone that is hasty in thoughts will tend only to lack! Once you have been able to identify your goals, you must engage in focused thinking to arrive at clarity of thought. Even when you need to multi-task, ensure you think through on one task at a time; this helps to ensure your perception is very precise. Start this day with clarity of purpose and goals and you will surely return with singing. Have a glorious day.

Day 30   Access to Divine Secrets

'Then Daniel went in, and desired of the king that he would give him time, and that he would show the king the interpretation' Dan. 2:16

King Nebuchadnezzar had a dream that terrified him, but he had forgotten the details when he woke up. He was so troubled that he was unable to sleep for days thereafter. So, he made a decree that all the wise men; the astrologers and soothsayers, would be killed if they could not interpret his dream. Nebuchadnezzar was correct in his assessment that the dream was grave. However, the fact that he expected the wise men to tell him the dream and the interpretation is callous! Daniel however went in and requested the king to give him time, after which he will give the dream and the interpretation!

I want to believe that this situation is applicable to you because there is a God in heaven that reveals secrets. The world is ruled from the realm of the spirit; it is those that have access to the reveller of secrets that will be able to decode the language that controls in the atmosphere. You as a believer have an advantage. As Daniel said, 'give me time', all you need is time to access the divine secrets.

Verse 22 says *'He reveals things that are deep and secret; he knows what is hidden in darkness, and he himself is surrounded by light'*! The light dwells with God and He knows what is in the darkness! I give you a challenge today; if you would spend time with the one that reveals all secretes, there is nothing that will be hidden from you. There will be nothing impossible for you – you will come out from your hiding with the light that will show you the direction to overcome all of life's issues.

Day 31   Choose to Think Good Thoughts

"Finally brethren, whatsoever things are true, whatsoever things are honest, whatsoever things are just, whatsoever things are pure, whatsoever things are lovely, whatsoever things are of good report; if there be any virtue, and if there be any praise, think on these things." Philippians 4:8.

Today, the Lord is giving to us clearly, what we should occupy our thoughts with. We should occupy our thoughts with truths, with honest, just, and pure information. We are instructed to occupy our minds with lovely thoughts, with good report, with things of great virtue, with things of praise.

What you think affects what you become. Proverbs 23:7 says, 'as a man thinketh in his heart so is he'. When your countenance is sad, it is because of what is on your mind. When you are thinking of impossibilities, you are likely to experience impossibilities. If you expect prayers to be answered, you must think on what the word of God says about the request you have brought before God. If you are trusting God for your healing, let your thoughts be filled with the honest report about your health; truth about your health.

The truth is in the word of God. So your challenge is to guard your, mind. If you want to live a pure life, think on truths that are in the word of God. Today, what you are requested to do is to think on the word of God. The result will be clear, your lifting will be evident and your profiting will appear to all. Guard your thoughts.

Day 32   Words of Life; Words of Health

My son, attend to my words; incline thine ear unto my saying. Let them not depart from thine eyes; keep them in the midst of thine heart. For they are life unto those that find them, and health to all their flesh" Proverbs 4:20-22

This scripture gives us simple but profound recipe for a life worth living. The summary of the instruction here is very clear; give the word undivided attention. 'Eat and Drink' the word. Open your ears to it, and close your ears to other sayings. Keep reading, and listening to the word. Keep them in your heart. Do all you need to do to ensure that you neither forget the word nor allow it to slip off from your mind!

The more attention you give the word, the higher the chances of 'finding' it. To 'find' here means, to make discoveries. You will discover the secrets to good life as you delve into the word each day. You will find health and healing in the word. You certainly will find relevant word that provides answers to every question life confronts you with. Search the word, then apply them, yield to them, and you will find solutions, healings, health and peace to your soul.

I strongly believe that the answer to whatever challenge life will bring your way today is in the word you already came across before. Think through and you will 'find' them. Determine to apply the word to every temptation or challenge that you will face today, and you will experience victory and peace.

Day 33   Watch What You Say

'Watch your words and hold your tongue, you would save yourself a lot of grief'. Proverbs 21:23 MSG

I have a great concern, for some people have been able to destroy their lives because of what they say. The good news version of today's scripture says: *'if you want to stay out of trouble, be careful what you say'*.

Sometime you spoke proudly and were not required to talk. Sometime you spoke against your spouse, and you could have just kept your mouth shut. Some other time, in your office, you decided to make a jest while you were not required to make one. Please keep your mouth shut if there is no need to speak, or if you cannot speak good words.

As you face the day, be careful what you say; at the coffee shop, at your job site, in your office, or as you cook the food for your family. As you return home to meet your spouse, be careful; don't just make a jest that will make him or her feel angry. Your marriage, your work, your relationship, can be preserved if you would take care in what you say daily.

Remember, *'whoever guards his mouth and tongue keeps his soul from troubles' (NKJV)*. I pray that mercy will reach unto you today, in Jesus name. Amen.

Day 34   Your Confession Makes or Mars Your Destiny

A man's belly shall be satisfied with the fruit of his mouth; and with the increase of his lips shall he be filled. Death and life are in the power of the tongue: and they that love it shall eat the fruit thereof.'
Proverbs 18:20-21

Every single moment, you have the opportunity to create your future by the word of your mouth. You have to be mindful of what you say. Your utterances can make or destroy your work, your marriage or even the future of your children. However bad the situations you face may look, you should not complicate them by the words that come out of your mouth.

Here are some examples; assuming you had a quarrel with your spouse, do not be so angry and tell yourself 'this is the end of the relationship'. Don't curse your children by negative declaration on them. Never make negative confession on your business. Your duty is to declare 'the good' you desire as declared in the word, not your perception. We walk by faith not by sight (2Cor 5:7).

Consider the message version of Pr. 18:20: *'Words satisfy the mind as much as fruit does the stomach; good talk is as gratifying as a good harvest'*. At least speak positive! Look at verse 21: *'words kill, words give life; they're either poison or fruit – you choose.'* So, YOU have to choose! Would you decide to give life to your future and that of your family, or you would give poison? I hope you choose to give life. Speak positive, speak right, speak the word; and God of heaven will back it up and He will bless you richly, in Jesus name.

Day 35   Give Word Expression to Your Faith

And Jesus answering saith unto them, Have faith in God. For verily I say unto you, That whosoever shall say unto this mountain, Be thou removed, and be thou cast into the sea; and shall not doubt in his heart, but shall believe that those things which he saith shall come to pass; he shall have whatsoever he saith. Mark 11:22-23

The word of God expressly states the desire and the promises of God for us to be well; to be prosperous, and to be in health even as our soul prospers. Isaiah 53:4-5; 1Peter 2:24; 3 John: 2. In spite of all these, Mark 11:23 says, however, that it will take us declaring with our mouth for these results to manifest.

After you have taken the time to pray about any issue in your life; be it health, wealth, marriage, business, or be it about your children; not only do you need to guard your thoughts and focus on what the word of God says about these issues, but it's also required of us to keep declaring what we believe. We must give verbal expressions to our faith and actively confess what we believe while we are waiting to see the physical manifestation. The Bible says you will have whatsoever you say.

Therefore it is not only the fact that God has promised that you will have it, or that the word has declared that you already have it, but until you speak it out of your mouth, having believed it in your heart, you might not see the manifestation. Therefore, believe and confess positively in line with God's word all the time and it shall come to pass, in the name of Jesus. God bless your day, amen.

Day 36   The Tongue of the Wise is Health

"There is that speaketh like the piercings of a sword: but the tongue of the wise is health."
Proverbs 12:18.

Your tongue should bring health if you are wise. This talks about your utterances. You can destroy or make alive your faith with what you say. Be determined to speak with your mouth only the words of faith and only the words that you believe in. And as you declare what you believe, health will come forth.

Proverbs 18:21 says that death and life are in the power of the tongue. It means you have to give a vote to which one wins. If you feel deadness in your body or in your mind in anyway, what you will declare in your mouth is not what you feel, it's what you believe. So your mouth can bring death to your circumstances, or your mouth can bring life. I have found out, both from the word of God and personal experience, that there is a need for us to declare with our mouth by faith. And the scripture says here in proverbs 12:18 that the wise man will declare in such a way that health will spring forth out of your physical body.

If you will stand and determine to speak health and wellness only, everything you prayed about will be fuelled. The wise man only speaks positively and would keep quiet when there is no good news to report. Death and life are in your tongue and the tongue of the wise gives health. May the lord bless your day today in Jesus name, amen.

Day 37   Speak What You Believe

> *"We having the same spirit of faith, according as it is written, I believed, and therefore have I spoken; we also believe, and therefore speak" 2 Corinthians 4:13*

The emphasis from this scripture is 'making declarations only of what you believe.' Only what you believe is to come out of your mouth. The Bible says here that we believe and so we speak. Your belief is important but your speaking is also very essential. If you betray yourself by talking about what you really don't believe or expect to happen, you nullify what you thought you believed. The bible for example, says that by the stripes of Christ you were healed and you wake up in the morning with a headache or you wake up in the morning with thoughts that caused fear to come to your mind. That is what you feel, but what you should speak is what you believe.

2 Corinthians 4:13 says *'we also believe and therefore have we speak'*. So if you do not yet have a depth of believe concretised in your mind, based on provisions in the word of God, about any issue you are facing, you have no business speaking. Invest some time to do some homework; get into the word about that situation in your life. Then you will have foundation to base your faith upon.

B We've been talking about prayer and thinking right but now we have to talk about declaring right and make sure that what you say is what you have always believed. May God bless your day in the name of Jesus.

Day 38   Keep Saying the Same Things

"Seeing then that we have a great high priest, that is passed into the heavens, Jesus the Son of God, let us hold fast our profession." Hebrews 4:14.

This is the most difficult part for a Christian walk, particularly when you are in the middle of a challenge. To maintain a positive confession or to keep confessing what you believe might be difficult because your feelings could override your heart at that point in time; but your work is to make sure that your heart and your confessions override your feelings.

The scripture says in verse 14, seeing then that we have a great high priest that is passed into the heavens, Jesus the Son of God let us hold fast our profession. The word profession there also means confession. Let us keep maintaining the faith that we have stood upon. Let's keep declaring what we have stood upon. This principle is what you need as a person to get to the next level. You have to speak what the God of heaven has said about you, your home, your business, etc.

You might even get negative feedback but you have to keep saying what you believe. So let us maintain our profession because it says we have a great high priest that is gone to heaven. What that means is that when he went up to heaven he actually finished what is required for you to get into your breakthrough. So settle that in your mind and keep saying the same thing that you have always believed. You will find that you will have whatever you say – it's only a matter of time! God bless your day, in Jesus name, amen.

Day 39   Results Come Only As You 'Say'

But what saith it? The word is nigh thee, even in thy mouth, and in thy heart: that is, the word of faith, which we preach; That if thou shalt confess with thy mouth the Lord Jesus, and shalt believe in thine heart that God hath raised him from the dead, thou shalt be saved. For with the heart man believeth unto righteousness; and with the mouth confession is made unto salvation" Romans 10:8-10.

With the heart you believe, while with the mouth confession is made that you may be saved.

The word saved doesn't just talk about salvation as when you believed in Jesus as your Lord and saviour, but it talks about deliverance from sin, sickness, and spiritual death. So if you want healing from sicknesses and mighty deliverances in any other area of your life; what this scripture is saying is that though you believe in your heart that God has done it or he is able to do it, it only comes to manifestation as you confess this with your mouth.

This principle is needed to be put in practice. And as you face your day today, make sure you put it into practice. What should come out of your mouth should be the source of deliverance for your life. You need to make utterances that will bring the manifestation of what you believe God for.

God is very clear in His word; you will only have results in your life as you declare with your mouth what you have believed from the word of God. May God bless your day in Jesus name, amen.

Day 40   God Quickens the Dead

"(As it is written, I have made thee a father of many nations,) before him whom he believed, even God, who quickeneth the dead, and calleth those things which be not as though they were." Romans 4:17

This is the description of the almighty God. He quickens the dead, and calls those things which are not as though they were.

God's principle of quickening the dead and calling those things that are not to be as though they were should become your principle too. This principle must determine what you think about. When situations are looking negative; remember this, God quickens the dead. That should be in your thoughts. All through the day, if anything is looking negative, always remember that the Bible says 'God calls those things that be not as though they were'. What should be in your thoughts is the fact that God will turn around the situation.

What should be in your thoughts is the fact that God quickens the dead, He brings life into deadness. That is what should be in your thoughts - the fact that God can turn around that dead circumstance and bring life into it. That is the nature of God. He quickens the dead, he brings hope to hopelessness, and He brings life to deadness.

Why don't you think about that? So don't ever think of any impossibility. Think of the power of possibilities that is held by the God that you serve. Today, you will experience breakthroughs in every area of your life in Jesus name. Think that way - and you will find it easy to 'talk that way'; and you will find lines falling unto you in pleasant places. Have a testimony-filled day.

Day 41   Don't Stagger

> *"He staggered not at the promise of God through unbelief; but was strong in faith, giving glory to God". Romans 4:20*

What has the Lord told you? Don't stagger at the promise. Do not stagger. Do not be distracted. Do not be discouraged. Do not give room for any thought of impossibility. Because Abram received God's promise, the thoughts of how dead his and his wife's bodies were and how old they were, did not make him stagger at the promise. What you're seeing today should not make you stagger at the promise of God concerning your life.

Look at verse 21, *"And being fully persuaded that, what he had promised, he was able also to perform."* Abram was persuaded! So, you too should rather be persuaded. Be convinced that God who promised will bring it to pass. Be persuaded. I don't have a doubt that you will experience your lifting. I don't have a doubt that the papers you are expecting are on the way.

Why don't you just believe God? Don't stagger at the promise. Don't stagger at His promise to you of a spouse. Remember, *'God sets the solitary in families' (Ps 68:6).* Don't stagger at the promise of promotion because the bible says *'they go from strength to strength' (Ps. 84:7)* and *'the path of the just is as a shining light' (Pr. 4:18).* Don't stagger because of the persistent pain, sound health is your portion (1Pet 2:24). Don't stagger at the delay of child birth, *'happy are they that have their quivers full of many children' (Ps. 127:3-5).* Don't stagger; great shall be your peace.

I give you a word of promise today according to the word of God. He that promised shall bring it to pass. Therefore be persuaded. May God bless your day in the name of Jesus, amen.

Day 42 Don't Consider Your Negative Situation

"And being not weak in faith, he considered not his own body now dead, when he was about an hundred years old, neither yet the deadness of Sara's womb". Romans 4: 19.

In Romans 4:19 the Lord is showing us the experience and the example of the faith that Abraham had. It says, 'being not weak in faith, he considered not his own body now dead'.

My focus today is on what you should not consider. Abram considered not his own body now dead, that's number 1. He did not consider also, that he was a hundred years of age, that's number 2. Number 3, Abraham did not consider the fact that Sarah's womb was dead. Consider not.

The fact that he did not consider does not mean he did not know. He was aware of this fact of medical report! He was aware of his situation. But he did not give it a consideration. His consideration was the word of God. His mind was filled with God's promise. That should be your attitude today. Do not consider any negative circumstance; give it no thought. You might have heard negative news; do not give it consideration over and above the good news that you know in the word.

Whatever you believe or trust God for. Let your thought be focused only on what the promise of the father is. Do not give consideration to all the bad information you have received about your wife, about your child, about your finances, about your health, or whatever else it is. Think on God's word. Consider the promise of your father. Do not consider the facts that look negative. God will give you peace today as you go in faith in Jesus name, amen.

Day 43   Consider Jesus

> *"Looking unto Jesus the author and finisher of our faith; who for the joy that was set before him endured the cross, despising the shame, and is set down at the right hand of the throne of God."*
> *Hebrews 12:2*

Today God is saying to us 'consider him'. Consider the person of Christ. When he went to the cross, think about what he did. That's what the word consider means. Consider what transpired when Jesus went to the cross.

Look at verse 3. *"For consider him that endured such contradiction of sinners against himself, lest ye be wearied and faint in your minds."* Now, each time you are thinking about how long you have waited for your breakthrough, the Bible says in Hebrews 12:3; *'consider him'*. Consider him; give thought to what the Lord has done. Give deep consideration to what Jesus has settled on the cross of Calvary.

The solution to all the circumstances that you face in your life has been settled on the cross of Calvary. That is what you should consider. Consider the fact that your sickness has been paid for, consider the fact that your sins have been paid for, consider the fact that the sacrifice on the cross is adequate to bring deliverance to your child, if only you can hold unto the blood that was shed on Calvary. Consider the fact that your sins are forgiven, consider the fact that circumstances may look negative but when Jesus went to the cross, he said "It is finished". Consider that. Give thought to it. So the devil must not distract you as you face your day, consider the Lordship of Jesus. Consider the finished work on Calvary, and great shall be your peace as you walk in faith today. You will return with rejoicing in the name of Jesus, amen.

Day 44   Whatever Happens, Do Not Panic

'These things have I spoken unto you, that in me ye may have peace. In the world ye have tribulation: but be of good cheer; I have overcome the world'. John 16:33 ASV (See this also in MSG and KJV)

These were the words of Jesus to His disciples in very difficult times when He was about to leave them. He is saying the same to you today – Whatever happens, stay united to me, Do Not Panic. If there was any time in history that we need these words from our Lord Jesus Christ, it is now!

In this chapter, Jesus was sort-of giving His disciples a farewell speech! You can remember that the disciples faced a lot of challenges after Jesus left them. Times are changing today too, situations are getting more difficult, economic downturns are all over the world. We are seeing more wars and hearing rumours of more wars! Earthquakes are happening more frequently and getting more devastating! Situations are becoming more unpredictable. But the Bible says here that you should be at peace in the midst of these negative circumstances.

Earlier in verses 7 and 8, Jesus told his disciples of the promised Comforter that He will send after He has gone! Today, we have the Comforter as our helper – He is in you to strengthen you as you go through every life's situation. Then in concluding this chapter, Jesus said 'be of good cheer, I have overcome the world'! Be rest assured in these two facts and do not entertain any panic in your heart, whatever you might be facing. Whatever the case may seem, never allow your heart to fear, do not panic! You are more than a conqueror. Do have a victorious day!

Day 45   There is a Door of Escape

"There hath no temptation taken you but such as man can bear: but God is faithful, who will not suffer you to be tempted above that ye are able; but will with the temptation make also the way of escape, that ye may be able to endure it." 1 Cor. 10:1 ASV

Whatever difficulty you might be confronted with in life, God allowed it to come your way knowing that you have the capacity to bear it while you figure out a way out of it! This might sound too simple and idealistic, but it is the bible truth! Every and anytime you face a challenge in life, be rest assured that there is a door of escape that the Lord has prepared for you to successfully go through it. You only need to look out for it!

What the devil would like you to think is that your end has come because of your temporary negative experience. But listen, God says there is a way out! God is faithful to make a way out for you, and to also show you that way. There is enough wisdom in God to unravel every riddle, untie every knot and deliver you from every trouble! With this truth secured in your heart; you can relax, look inwards and listen to the Holy Spirit to show you the secret to the challenge you might be currently faced with.

Determine to acknowledge God, and not lean to your own understanding. There is a door of escape for you: to pay the debt; to be free from the court case; to get out of sickness; to overcome temptation; to be delivered form that overwhelming situation! Say this with me now, 'I know there is a divine way out of this situation that I am faced with (mention out the situation), and in Jesus name, I receive the understanding of what to do, Amen.' So shall it be, in Jesus name.

Day 46   Hope in His Mercy

'Let Israel hope in the Lord: for with the Lord there is mercy, and with him is plenteous redemption. And he shall redeem Israel from all his iniquities.' Ps. 130:7-8

You can have hope in the midst of challenges – no matter how terrible things look. Why? Because in God, there is mercy – plenty of mercies! Wow, this is great news! Your hope in God during your trying times is not based on how good you are, but how merciful God is! NIV version of verse seven says, 'for with the Lord is unfailing love'. Even when your trouble is due to your errors, you can still approach God for help, based on His unfailing love!

So; maintain your hope in the Lord, because there is mercy with Him. God will redeem you from ALL your troubles if you would turn to Him and make a demand on the offer of His mercy. There is a way out of every situation that looks impossible to man. As you face the day, may you encounter the mercies of God in all your situations, in Jesus name.

Day 47   Be Strong and Courageous

> *"Be strong, be courageous, all you that hope in the LORD." Ps. 31: 24 GNB*
>
> *"Be strong, and let your heart take courage, all ye that hope in Jehovah." Ps. 31: 24 ASV*
>
> *"Be brave. Be strong. Don't give up. Expect GOD to get here soon." Ps. 31: 24 MSG*
>
> *"Be of good courage, and he shall strengthen your heart, all ye that hope in the LORD." Ps. 31: 24 KJN*

When your hope in the Lord is strong, you will remain strong and courageous. The worst battle you can fight in any situation of life is the loss of hope. Whatever you face today, determine to stay in hope in your God. Don't ever give up; He will soon appear with the desires of your heart.

The Message bible says: 'Be brave', keep moving positively – on, in the face of the challenges and oppositions, 'Don't give up'; the Lord will show forth for you soon, in Jesus name. You must have heard the phrase 'courage is not an absence of fear'; so, despite how scary the situations you face might be, summon all the courage you need from the strength of your hope in God and His word. Look at God's promises again about that situation, declare them to yourself confidently, and be courageous as you wait for the Lord to show up – He sure will. May the Lord give you reasons to sing a new song of testimonies shortly. In Jesus name, you are blessed of the Lord.

Day 48   You Will Sing Victory Song
Today

> *"You are my hiding place; you will save me from trouble. I will sing aloud of your salvation, because you protect me." Ps. 32:7 GNB*
>
> *"Thou art my hiding-place; thou wilt preserve me from trouble; Thou wilt compass me about with songs of deliverance. Selah" Ps. 32:7 ASV*

The key word this morning is; 'God is your hiding place'. As you go through the day, the Lord says 'He will give you a song of deliverance'. Therefore, be sure that He will save you from trouble, and He will encompass you with songs of deliverance. Whatever your mission today; may be you are going for an exam, an interview, a business deal, to your normal place of work, or you are going for a ministration. You might even be envisaging a confrontation in the course of the day. As you face the day, this should be your word of confession. 'I will sing victory song today, in Jesus name'.

The Bible says, 'and they shall return unto Zion with singing, and everlasting song shall be upon their lips'. As you face the market place today, determine to save yourself from the battle of anxiety, because the Lord says He will save you from all trouble. He will encompass you with songs of deliverance. For every battle you might be facing, God is saying to you that at the end of the day, you will sing the song of victory. That is my prayer for you, and so shall it be, in Jesus name. Go in peace, and be blessed.

Day 49   The Mercy of God

'There is no king saved by the multitude of a host: a mighty man is not delivered by much strength. A horse is a vain thing for safety: neither shall he deliver any by his great strength. Behold, the eye of the Lord is upon them that fear Him, upon them that hope in His mercy'   Ps. 33:16-18

In our scripture reading today, you will notice that human source of strength is not adequate to deliver when trouble comes. You therefore cannot depend on your own ability. In the same vein, you need not be in despair because of your inabilities. In most cases, our confidence is on our ability to pray, and may be on the fact that we have great faith! However, if we would learn to approach the Lord on the platform of his mercy, there will certainly be a light at the end of every tunnel we find ourselves.

You might have a family problem, or a case pending in court, ask God for His mercy; if you have any trouble in the marketplace, you just need to ask God to show you mercy. Remember this; a horse is vain thing in the day of battle, there is no king that is saved by the multitude of a host.

Whoever you might know, whatever you might have is not your source of safety. Whichever area of life you need help, ask God to show you His mercy, let your dependence be solely on him, and as you cry unto Him in faith, you will experience the divine assistance that you need. May you experience the mercies of God in all that you lay your hands upon to do today, in Jesus name. Amen.

Day 50   To Deliver Your Soul from Death

'Behold, the eye of the Lord is upon them that fear
Him, upon them that hope in His mercy; to deliver
their soul from death, and to keep them alive in
famine' Ps. 33:18-19

This scripture fascinates and refreshes me each time I read it.
God's eyes are upon those that hope in his mercy! When the
Lord sets His eyes upon a man to show him mercy, you will
agree with me that that person is well secured all the times.
Verse 19 clearly states what God's mercy will accomplish in
their lives and situation: a) to deliver their soul from death; b)
to keep them alive in famine. The word 'deliver' here literarily
mean 'to snatch away' or 'to rescue'. And the word 'death'
could also represent any kind of 'pestilence', 'disaster' or
'ruin'. Life is full of negative situations – and God is giving
you an assurance for safety – if you will only hope in His
mercy! When you are faced with life's hopeless situations and
you feel helpless, you can cry unto God for mercy, and He will
send His deliverance and enlargement!

Your challenge could be in the area of health, finances, or
marriage. Once, the Jews were faced with the crises of
imminent extermination; they cried unto God with fasting. God
showed them His favour and sent deliverance and enlargement
to them. (Esther 3 to 10). God will do the same for you today.
Whatever your challenges, call upon God NOW – tell Him 'Oh
Lord, have mercy on me, for I hope in your mercy'. The Lord
will deliver your soul from your troubles today, in Jesus name.
Amen.

Day 51 Your Help and Shield

> *'Our soul waiteth for the Lord: he is our help and shield' Ps. 33:20*

I pray for you today that God will give you understanding and grant you access to in-depth revelation and insight about the power and efficacy of God's mercy. This will help you to experience the best of God in your Christian walk. God's help will enhance you to move ahead in life, while as your shield, He will defend you from any battle that may want to confront you in any area of life. When you focus on God, this will be your experience. The psalmist says *'some trust in chariots and some in horses, but we will remember the name of the Lord our God'* (Ps. 20:7).

When you put your trust in the Lord, you position yourself to have access to the totality of God's power and ability. His help becomes available to you; and He defends you from all troubles in life. Psalm 20:8 says while others are brought down and fall, you are arisen and stand upright. Praise the Lord! I like the good news version of today's scripture *'we put our hope in the Lord; he is our protector and our help'*.

This is a new day for you, yesterday's challenge has passed, but His new mercy today will help you overcome every new challenge. The mercy of God brings forgiveness of sins, and delivers you from the cases that you think are too difficult for you to handle. In fact, God's mercy, when in effect, actually delivers you from going through the challenges that you should have gone through due to your fault – this is what mercy does! Whatever you might have as a challenge today, God is offering you His help, based on His mercy.

Day 52   Lord Let Your Mercy Be upon Me

*'Let thy mercy O Lord, be upon us, according as
we hope in thee'. Ps. 33:22*

This is a key prayer you can and should pray as you face each
day. This way, you set yourself for daily victory, and I am sure
God's mercy is still available! Let's pray right away – 'let your
mercy O Lord be upon me because as I hope in you'!

This scripture establishes a condition of experiencing God's
mercies – Amplified version says *'in proportion to our waiting
and hoping for You'* ('You' here meaning God). You might
have a financial burden on your neck, or needs of any kind – as
you pray this, and you patiently wait on God for divine
intervention, all your anxiety will be taken care of. Listen;
grace is unmerited favour, i.e. you will obtain favour that you
do not deserve; whereas mercy will prevent you from suffering
what you were doomed to suffer! So, mercy averts whatever
difficult things that was due to come upon you.

The problem with which you are currently faced, which might
even have been caused by yourself, and your mind is telling
you that you deserve to face the consequence; but I tell you
today that God's mercy will deliver you as you put your hope
in Him. Approach the Lord today with all your anxieties, hope
in Him, and He is literally saying to you 'my mercy will reach
unto you – even today'! Receive the manifestation of His
mercy today, in Jesus name.

Day 53   His Mercy Brings Forgiveness

*'For I will be merciful to their unrighteousness,
and their sins and their iniquities will I remember
no more'. Heb. 8:12*

This scripture states clearly that no one is too bad to experience
God's mercy. Sometimes we are not confident enough to
approach God and ask him to show us mercy, all because we
think we have done too much bad to deserve God's help – and
rightly so, is this your situation? From today's scripture, what
your unrighteousness would have brought upon you in form of
calamity, God is saying 'His mercy will wade-in and overlook
it'. What good news!

It does not matter how deep you have been in error, sin, or
wickedness of any kind, if you would turn to the Lord and say
'Lord I come to you just as I am, show me mercy and
forgiveness'.

Mercy is available for us because God remembers the blood
that Jesus shed on the cross for us (Heb. 4:14-16). That blood
still speaks today! You become qualified for God's mercy, no
matter what unrighteousness you did; and you obtained mercy
and forgiveness. You just need to make a fresh commitment
with the Lord now that you will follow Him all the remaining
days of your life, and you can begin your life afresh on a clean
slate.

Today, God is releasing His mercy on your health, marriage,
career, or ministry. Now, based on your positive response to
today's scripture, confront the devil in faith and cast out every
sense of guilt and condemnation. Today is a new beginning for
you in God. Face your future in faith and confidently. It is well
with you in Jesus name. Amen.

Day 54 O Satisfy Us Early with Your Mercy

'O satisfy us early with thy mercy; that we may rejoice and be glad all our days.' Ps. 90:14

Each day you are alive, your heart longs for the fulfilment of some desire! What brings the happiness and the sense of satisfaction in your heart would defer from that of another. Whatever your daily aspirations though, you can only experience satisfaction by the mercies of God.

It does not matter how many good things of life man can possess, or how long she/he might live; the most important question to ask is 'are you satisfied with the mercies of God, to the extent that you rejoice and you are glad everyday'? If you are living each day in sorrow or with heavy burden at the back of your mind, then you are not satisfied! It does not matter how long you live, or how much earthly goods you possess; you could be married and yet unsatisfied; highly placed in the society, and yet lonely and internally frustrated!

Despite the acclaimed wisdom of Solomon, and after all the great accomplishments and earthly goods and pleasure he enjoyed, he said *'yet, when I surveyed all that my hands have done and what I had toiled to achieve, everything was meaningless, a chasing after the wind; nothing was gain under the sun'* (Eccl. 2:11, NIV). So, if you are lacking in joy and satisfaction today, don't be discouraged – there is yet hope for you. Do what the psalmist did – cry out unto God, not for the 'things' you think you lack, but cry out to God to 'satisfy you with His mercy' that you might rejoice and be glad all your remaining days on earth. God bless you with peace, in Jesus name. Amen.

Day 55   It Is Not Too Late – Look Unto Him Again!

> *Then Jonah prayed unto the Lord his God out of the fish's belly, And said, I cried by reason of mine affliction unto the Lord, and he heard me; out of the belly of hell cried I, and thou heardest my voice. ³For thou hast cast me into the deep, in the midst of the seas; and the floods compassed me about: all thy billows and thy waves passed over me. ⁴Then I said, I am cast out of thy sight; yet I will look again toward thy holy temple.*   *Jonah 2:1-4*

If you are familiar with the story of Jonah; how he ran away from the Lord in disobedience, you would probably not be too surprised that he ended up in the belly of the fish, in the depth of the sea! That would have been his end, but for God. I believe it was mercy that found Jonah and gave him another chance.

You might be in the position of Jonah today – may be you ran away from His presence, from His will for your life; and all hell broke loose against you, I am telling you today that there is yet hope for you. Mercy is still available to you today. Consider what Jonah said in verse 4, 'then I said, I am cast out of thy sight; yet I will look again towards thy holy temple'.

Please take courage and look again towards the throne of grace, and you will find the help you need. Dare to arise in hope, approach the presence of God by the everlasting Blood of Jesus Christ and seek God in prayer again. I am sure that God will do you good, and your mouth will be filled with testimonies, in Jesus name, amen.

Day 56   Thanksgiving in the Belly of Hell!

But I will sacrifice unto thee with the voice of thanksgiving; I will pay that that I have vowed. Salvation is of the Lord And the Lord spake unto the fish, and it vomited out Jonah upon the dry land'. Jonah 2:9-10

You would remember from yesterday's devotionals that 'Jonah looked again' unto the Lord in prayer.

He described his situation as one being in hell! Yet he could summon courage and hope to cry unto God, and he obtained mercy and found grace. I noticed however in verse 9 that his calamitous situation was not finally turned around until he turned the gear of his prayers to thanksgiving!

When your thanksgiving and praises goes up, heaven comes down to your situation. Bible says, the Lord inhabits the praise of His people, and anywhere the Lord inhabits experiences fullness of joy. You might have been praying and praying in hope, without any visible positive change in your situation; you now need to turn the gear to thanksgiving and praise unto God.

Remember Paul and Silas. They prayed, yes, but they sang praises too. They were so bold at it that in spite of their situation in the prison, they kept praising God aloud such that all their prison colleagues heard them! Their faith was loud and clear through their praises! The heavens showed up, and everyone in the prison partook of the power of deliverance. If you can dare to praise God in your 'belly of hell', the word of the Lord will come forth and the fish will vomit you – from the depth of the seas to your dry land, in Jesus name. Amen.

Day 57   On Whose Side Are You?

'And it came to pass, when Joshua was by Jericho, that he lifted up his eyes and looked, and behold, there stood a man over against him with his sword drawn in his hand: and Joshua went unto him, and said unto him, Art thou for us, or for our adversaries? And he said, Nay; but as captain of the host of the Lord am I come. And Joshua fell on his face to the earth, and did worship, and said unto him, what saith my lord unto his servant?' Joshua 5:13-14

The man with the sword here had been sent to take charge of the command of the army of God! Think about it. He is neither for Israel nor against Israel, he came to fulfil a divine mandate! Joshua's response is insightful – what do you say to your servant?!

Many times when we are faced with challenges of life, we usually expect God to move in ways we can imagine or see, or used to; but that is not always God – He works in ways we cannot see. Pr. 3:5 says, *'Trust in the Lord; and lean not unto thine own understanding'*. Verse 7 says *'Be not wise in your own eyes'*!

Our response should be like Joshua – fall in line behind the Lord of Host. Tell Him 'Lord, what do you say to your servant?' At such time, stick with the instructions or promises in God's word about the situation, and make it your decision. Make up your mind to be on God's side at such time, and victory is certain for you. Imagine, it was in that disposition that God released to them the word of victory (Josh. 6:1-2) – *'See, I have given into your hand Jericho, and the king and the mighty men'*!

Day 58   The Lord Is My Shepherd

*The Lord is my Shepherd [to feed, guide, and shield
me], I shall not lack.   He makes me lie down in
[fresh, tender] green pastures; He leads me beside
the still and restful waters. Ps. 23:1-2 AMP*

Psalm 23 is a very interesting and rich poem of David. You
would recall that David himself was a shepherd boy; his father
Jesse had left him in charge of the flock when he was a small
boy. David recounted to King Saul how God helped him to
protect the sheep while he fought and won against a lion and a
beer. David declared: the same God that helped him that time
will certainly deliver him from the hands of Goliath! (1 Sam
17: 32 – 37).

David knew the role of a Shepherd. A Shepherd feeds, guides
and protects the sheep. David also particularly had his faith
built on the fact that his own Shepherd is God. He trusts the
Lord to feed, guide and protect him. I like the way Living bible
version puts it in verse 1: *'Because the Lord is my Shepherd, I
have everything I need'*! Note the key word here: Because.
David's confidence is in the person of The Lord.

If you will make the Lord your God, if you would put your
complete trust in Him as your shepherd, you can be rest
assured that you will be fully satisfied, and you will certainly
dwell in safety and victory. As a child of God, get to know
your God and you will be strong and do great exploits (Dan
10:32). The Lord our God is mighty; put your trust in Him and
you can rest assured in Him. If you have not yet accepted Jesus
as your Lord and saviour; decide to give Him your life today,
and you will find rest for your soul. (Matt 11:28 - 30)

Day 59   The Evil of Fear of Man

'The fear of man brings a snare: but whoever trusts in the Lord shall be safe' Pr. 29:25 NKJV

I like this scripture in the Good News Bible, *'It is dangerous to be concerned with what others think of you, but if you trust the Lord, you are safe'.*

Man is usually faced with the temptation of considering the opinion of others about our lives and the steps we take over and above God's word to us. Put in another way – 'what would people say'? Many are unable to put their whole trust in the Lord. They are concerned that people will consider them to be 'stupid' for trusting in the Lord; or for making decisions based on God's word and direction. Does that describe you?

Our scripture reading today states very clearly that only if you trust in the Lord are you sure of safety! Common English Bible version puts this verse this way – *'people are trapped by their fear of others; those who trust the Lord are secure'.* To be ensnared by what man would say, to the extent that you can't trust God completely would actually be a sin against God – God hates it when we compare Him with man!

Many times we know that God is leading us in a particular direction, but because it does not make common sense to us, and probably opposed to the view of someone we consider important, we are unable to go all out and obey God. This is being ensnared by the fear of man. This could be in the area of service to God, family matters, business concerns, or what have you. Think about it well right now as it relates to you; do you think you need to make amends in this regards? Then do so NOW! Never be ensnared by the fear of man's opinion. God bless your day.

Day 60   When I Am Really Afraid…

*'When I get really afraid I come to you in trust' Ps.
56:3 MSG*

Life is full of challenges and we are often faced with many
uncertain circumstances. To say that we do not sometimes, or
even often, get confronted with fearful situations would not be
completely correct. Whoever you are; however rich you are,
whatever age you are, as long as you are still in this world, the
chances are high that you have and will still face some
circumstances that will really make you afraid. The good news
is that the bible tells us what to do.

What struck me in this verse is the word 'when'! It did not say
'if'. This presents a dimension of certainty that we will face
situations in life that will make us to be really afraid!
Interestingly, the psalmist simply stated what he does when he
is confronted with real fear – he simply comes to God in trust!
We simply need to do the same when we are faced with real
fearful situations.

The key word here is 'Trust'. It is a noun, and it is defined as
'reliance on the integrity, strength, ability, surety, etc. of a
person or thing; confidence'. The dictionary goes ahead to
present it this way - 'a person on whom or thing on which one
relies: God is my trust'. What an appropriate example!

Therefore, when you are really afraid, come to God
confidently, knowing of certainty that He is well able to deliver
you from your problem, whatever it is, and however big and
scary it might be. When you are faced with life issues, tell
yourself and the situation, 'God is my trust, therefore I will not
fear'. God bless you. Amen.

Day 61   Prayer Opens Your Heaven

When all the people were baptized, it came to pass that Jesus also was baptized; and while He prayed, the heaven was opened. Luke 3:21 NKJV

Prayer is the gateway to peace in life. In this scripture, the bible says "the Heaven open upon Jesus as He prayed!" If you would cultivate the habit of starting your day in prayer – however way you know to – heaven will perpetually be open unto you and you will receive direction from the Lord and the required wisdom to tackle the issues that face you in the day.

In Mark 1:35-37, Jesus went out very early in the morning, into a solitary place, to pray. He always needed to meet people's needs and he was always able to meet their needs when 'All men sought Him'! It was however His custom to spend time alone with God first!

Start your day well, start with communion with the Lord in prayer and you will be on top of all issues of life that face you today.

Day 62   Do Not Fret About Anything!

Do not fret or have any anxiety about anything, but in every circumstance and in everything, by prayer and petition (definite requests), with thanksgiving, continue to make your wants known to God. Phil 4:6 AMP

Each day is full of different challenges. The answer to all troubles and challenges of life is in the place of prayer. The Lord however is telling us today from this scripture not to fret about anything. Clearly stated in the word, Do Not Be Anxious about Anything! Nothing is qualified to get you fretted or anxious! Absolutely nothing! Not your bad dream or nightmare; not your sickness, nor the trouble with your child. Not the troubles at work or in your business or ministry. Not even a national disaster!

Commit your day to the Lord in prayer, and go forth in faith and confidence. As you face the day, let nothing that comes up cause you to fret. Remain In the spirit of prayer and in faith, it is well with you, in Jesus name. Remember; your attitude in the place of prayer or after praying should be void of anxiety.

Day 63   Don't Be Anxious - Bring Every Trouble to the Lord

In nothing be anxious; but in everything by prayer and supplication with thanksgiving let your requests be made known unto God. Phil 4:6 ASV

This scripture says clearly: "In EVERYTHING by PRAYER". Every situation you face should be confronted with prayer. Not weeping, nor sighing, murmuring, complaining, arguing, shouting, agitation, or any or such things! Every trouble should be responded to by prayer. Stop acting otherwise! Pray. That is the method God expects you to respond.

James 5:13 says *"Is any among you afflicted, let him pray..."* That should be your first attitude; always.

What the devil wants is for you to cry, roll on the ground and think or say things that are not faith. Your first reaction should be – I will pray; I will talk to my father God. So, right now, pray about the issues, and supplicate if necessary; and keep thanking God. May God grant you a fulfilling day, in Jesus name.

Day 64   Let God Have All the Concern

Casting the whole of your care [all your anxieties, all your worries, all your concerns, once and for all] on Him, for He cares for you affectionately and cares about you watchfully. 1 Peter 5:7 AMP

When you have prayed, leave all the concern to the Lord. Believe the Lord completely, and let Him worry about the whole situation. This is one principle of effective praying. When you have been obedient in responding to all issues of life in prayer, let the God to whom you have prayed carry the burden. You must learn to maintain an anxiety free attitude from that moment onwards.

In I Samuel Chapter 1, Hanna prayed unto God for a child, she even wept bitterly because of the problem (V9-15). She ensured she asked specifically for a Boy. The bible says when she left the presence of the Lord; her countenance was 'no more sad' (V18). She allowed God to handle all the worries! The Result – She received the petition that she asked of the Lord – (V27).

Phil 4:6 tells us to let our request be made known unto God with thanksgiving. As you rise up from your place of prayer and face the day today, do not let your countenance to be sad! Walk and talk in faith. Ask with thanksgiving, and maintain an attitude of praise. The Lord is able – you will testify. May God grant you a fulfilling day, in Jesus name.

Day 65   Prayer Brings Peace

*Be careful for nothing; but in everything by prayer
and supplication with thanksgiving let your requests
be made known unto God. And the peace of God,
which passeth all understanding, shall keep your
hearts and minds through Christ Jesus. Phil 4:6-7*

Our focus in the last four days has been on prayer. Prayer is as
vital to you as breath is vital to life. Prayer is the answers to
every of life's issues. The Lord made it clear that we should
not fret at the face of any trouble. Rather, take it to the Lord in
prayer.

Verse 7 of today's scripture makes it clear that when we pray,
we will experience the peace of God that passes all
understanding. You might not be able to put your finger at the
solution yet; but God's peace will envelope you, if you can
pray.

Ps 46:10 says: *"Be at peace in the knowledge that I am
God..."* (BBE). When you have prayed in faith, relax; be at
peace in the knowledge of the fact that your God is God. He
will glorify Himself in the situation of your life, in Jesus name.

I declare unto you right now, receive the peace of God that
passes all understanding, in Jesus name. Your day will be
fruitful and peaceful in Jesus name. Amen.

Day 66   Don't Be Carried Away with Worries

> *'Therefore I say unto you, take no thought for your life what ye shall eat, or what ye shall drink; nor yet for your body, what ye shall put on. Is not the life more than meat, and the body than raiment?'* Matt. 6:25

The act of worry, as natural as it seems considering today's prevailing circumstances, is a clear sign that we thought that we are able in ourselves to handle every issue we face in life, such that the feeling of unpredictability leaves us in desperation! However, Matt. 6:27 raises a very important question *'which of you by taking thought can add one cubit to your stature?'* The answer is clear – none of us!

Worry does not solve any problems. On the other hand, for the believer, your life is hid with Christ in God (Col. 3:3). This should be a refreshing reminder to us, no matter what is happening in the world around us, God has you totally and properly covered. Verse 30 of that scripture goes further to state clearly that if God could clothe the ordinary grass of the field, how would you think he won't clothe you?!

You and I need to make a quality decision NOT TO WORRY about anything. It is wisdom not to worry. Worry kills and chokes life out of people. Worry will even sometimes make you take wrong steps that further complicate the situation you face. Rather, commit all your concerns to the Lord, and do not take them unto yourself. I pray that the Lord deliver you from all the things that are currently the reason for your worries, in Jesus name. Amen. Have a great day!

Day 67   God Has a Plan for Your Life

Before I formed thee in the belly I knew thee; and before thou camest forth out of the womb I sanctified thee, and I ordained thee a prophet unto the nations. Jeremiah 1:5

The message version of this scripture says *"Before I shaped you in the womb, I knew all about you."* I would like you to take time and think about this. It doesn't matter who your parents are currently, or the experiences you've had in life until this moment; this is God's word for you, and it is wisdom for you to believe it with all your heart. Notice the word 'I' - that is God speaking. Before I (God) shaped you in the womb, I (God) knew all about you.

Note the following points:

1. It was God who shaped you in the womb, you only came through your parents - they are vessels that God has used. Don't hate yourself. Don't hate your origin, but thank God for your life and your heritage.

2. Before He shaped you in the womb, God knew you. You may look insignificant right now in the earth, yet God knows what his plans are for you. God knew your end product before he started the process of your making.

3. God has a definite plan for your life. Stop wondering what your future will be like; go back to your creator and find out clearly from Him.

Stop being sad about what you've gone through so far, there is a plan behind your future - relax in God's hands. Your life will be better if you take some time to think about these facts. May God bless your day in Jesus name, Amen.

Day 68   You Are Not A Mistake

*I will praise thee; for I am fearfully and wonderfully
made: marvellous are thy works; and that my soul
knoweth right well. Ps. 139:14*

The message version of this verse says 'I thank you, High God
— you're breath-taking! Body and soul, I am marvellously
made! I worship in adoration — what a creation!' In the New
International version it says, 'I praise you because I am
fearfully and wonderfully made. Your works are wonderful, I
know that full well'.

Beloved I'd like you to understand today that the Lord wants
you to realize and appreciate the fact that you are beautifully
and wonderfully made. You are not a mistake; you did not get
here on earth, wherever you are right now, by chance. In the
message version it says you were sculptured from nothing into
something, you were woven together (verse 15). The new King
James Version says you were skilfully wrought. God knew you
long before you were conceived in your mother's womb and
God made you for a purpose.

Your soul must know and accept this fact. The Psalmist says,
"I worship in adoration- what a creation". Many people are
struggling with life today because they have not embraced the
fact that they were wonderfully and specially made by God. So
you must rejoice because God purposely created you. You
must think about your life in this way. Even if it looks like you
are nothing today, think again; God made you purposely, and
you are beautiful!

May God bless your day as you give a thought to this in Jesus'
name, amen.

Day 69   God's Thought for You

For I know the thoughts that I think toward you,
saith the Lord, thoughts of peace, and not of evil, to
give you an expected end. Then shall you call upon
me, and ye shall go and pray to me, and I will
harken to you. Jer. 29:11-12

I believe it is not by chance that you are reading this devotional right now. God says 'I know the thought that I think towards you'. Imagine that God is thinking about you – yes, YOU! Note that God's thoughts are not of evil, but of peace. His thoughts are designed to give you a future and a hope - to take you to an expected end. So, let fear be far from you. Even when events and people's comments have made you feel like a hopeless person. It is what God is saying that you should accept, think on, and take to heart.

His thought about you is that you will have a better life. Look at it in Message version *'...I know what I am doing. I have it all planned out – plans to take care of you, not to abandon you, plans to give you the future you hope for'*. Let your hope rise.

When you are confused about life; and people make you think like a hopeless person, remember this fact, and as you do, you will have better understanding. So, don't run your life by yourself, get back to the maker of your destiny – he promises to listen. Look at verse 12 in Message version 'when you call on me, when you come and pray to me, I'll listen'. Why don't you go to Him if you are confused, He will listen and reveal afresh to you His thought for you. There is light at the end of the tunnel for your great future. It is well with you, and may God bless your day, in Jesus name. Amen.

Day 70   Get to Know God's Plan for You

My people are destroyed for lack of knowledge:
because thou hast rejected knowledge, I will also
reject thee, that thou shalt be no priest to me: seeing
thou hast forgotten the law of thy God, I will also
forget thy children. Hosea 4:6

God sculpted you, and made you beautifully – He has a plan
for you that He has made even before you were formed in your
mother's womb. Even when you are confused about your life,
In Jer. 29:12, God said, when you come to me and you pray to
me I will listen! It does not matter who you are – either you
have accepted Christ as your saviour or not; or even if you
have made many mistakes in your journey of faith and have
walked away from God. You could have made 'booboos' of
your life as some people would say; if you come back to God,
He will still connect you to His original divine plans for you.

Hosea 4:6 says 'people are ruined because they lack knowledge
of God's plan for their lives'. That scripture makes it clear that
you will only be rejected or destroyed if you refuse God's
divine plan for your life. Get to seek God's plan for your life,
and you will not live a frustrated life.

I believe what God is saying is 'I really desire you to
remember my word, my will and my plans for your life'. The
only reason why you will be frustrated in life is if you do not
get back to God and His plans for your life; and not because He
is not accepting you. His hands are open today – get back to
God and His plans and He will reconnect you with His destiny
for you. God bless your day in Jesus name.

Day 71   Get God's Vision for Your Life

'Where there is no vision, the people perish: but he
that keepeth the law, happy is he' Proverbs 29:18
'Where there is no revelation, people cast off
restraint; but blessed is the one who heeds
wisdom's instruction.' Proverbs 29:18 NIV

The word 'vision' talks about redemptive revelation - an
understanding of God's plan and purpose. Vision is the ability
to see the desire, dream and goals that God has crafted ahead
for you before they exist in the natural.

The word 'perish' mean 'to cast off restrain', or to live
anyhow, unguarded, unfocused and an undisciplined life. So,
where there is no understanding of God's plan and purpose,
people live in an indiscipline way! That's why God is
challenging you to seek His divine plan for your life. Jer. 29:11
makes it clear that God has a clear and definite plan for every
aspect of your life, which He has laid out before you were
formed in your mother's womb. In fact, you were fearfully and
wonderfully sculptured to suit this plan.

Therefore, it is important that you devote appropriate time to
seek this divine plan. It is when you know God's plan for every
aspect of your life that you will be able to pursue it right. As a
businessman for example, you will beat about the bush in
business until you understand God's plan for your business.
This is true for every one about every area of life – home,
health, etc. If you would therefore invest time to discover this
plan, and you follow it, you will experience God's peace and
arrive at His expected end for you, in Jesus name, amen.

Day 72   Be Faithful

*Like the cold of snow [brought from the mountains]
in the time of harvest, so is a faithful messenger to
those who send him; for he refreshes the life of his
masters. Proverbs 25:13 AMP*

This scripture says a faithful messenger refreshes the life of their masters. To be faithful is to be loyal, trustworthy, constant, and reliable. Faithfulness is a person's attribute that can make him/her be preferred over a contemporary or an opposition.

Prov. 20:6 says *'Most men will proclaim everyone his own goodness: but a faithful man who can find?* Here is the question; are you a faithful worker, can your boss rely on you? When he is able, then we could say that you bring refreshing to his/her life. Otherwise, you bring a hurt. Nobody wants to have someone that will be a pain in the neck!

You might be diligent, very good – excellent in all you do. But if you are not trustworthy, it negates all your other qualities and your loyalty is in question. If the boss leaves the office and has some doubt on your faithfulness and your total commitment, in spite of your skill and diligence, then there is a lot in question about your life. A faithful person can also be described as a 'constant' person.

Also, can your spouse describe you as being faithful? Would God say you are a faithful person?

As you begin your day today, I encourage you, be faithful; bring refreshing to your employer, to your spouse, to your friend, and to God. If you do, great shall be your reward.

God bless your day, in Jesus name. Amen

Day 73   Be Loyal

A faithful man shall abound with blessings, but he who makes haste to be rich [at any cost] shall not go unpunished. Proverbs 28: 20 AMP

If you would find wisdom in being faithful, you will find wealth. A faithful man shall abound with blessings. I Cor. 4:2 also state clearly; *'it is required of a man to be faithful'*. If you are found to be faithful in stewardship, you will experience the reward of faithfulness. There is reward in being faithful.

As an employee, your boss is depending on you. Do not serve with the intention of stealing their business ideas and running with it.

Be faithful where you are serving right now, because you will abound with plenty when it is time to start your own. What does it mean to be faithful? Be loyal to them, be trustworthy, be dependable - be there for them. Don't be in a hurry for your time, because you can't draw the time closer by yourself. Your time will come; when it comes you will abound with plenty. Be faithful, be loyal, your future will be sustained if you do that.

Determine to cultivate this character in your life – at home, at work and in Church. May God bless your day, in the name of Jesus, amen.

Day 74   Decide to Bring Refreshing to Your Employer

A wicked messenger falleth into mischief: but a faithful ambassador is health. Proverbs 13:17

A wicked messenger falls into evil, but a faithful ambassador brings healing. Proverbs 13:17AMP

You will find here two categories of messengers – A wicked messenger and a faithful ambassador. From this scripture, the point being stressed is: When somebody is not faithful, he is being wicked! You can ask yourself again: are you a faithful or a wicked messenger? Are you faithful to your boss? If you are not loyal or dependable – not having your boss or the system in which you serve at heart, then you are not faithful – you are a wicked person.

If you are an employer and you notice unfaithfulness in any of your employees, don't waste your time, call the person immediately to address this issue. Do not waste your time keeping an unfaithful worker in your staff. If you are an employee, I employ you today to be faithful. Decide to bring health to your boss or the system in which you serve. This is wisdom.

Many people today have ruined their future because they wounded the place where they served and when their future came they also got wounded. Think about this.

Life is about seed time and harvest; as a matter of fact, life in itself is a seed! Decide today to be a healer, to bring refreshing, by being loyal; by being faithful, and you will reap it in future. May God bless you, in Jesus name. Have a great day.

Day 75   A Wise Servant Is Honoured As One Of The Family

'A wise servant shall have rule over a son that causeth shame, and shall have part of the inheritance among the brethren' Proverbs 17:2

There are two things to note from this verse of scripture – parents are challenged to be faithful in raising their children, not to become unruly such that they cause shame; while a servant or a worker is encouraged to be so faithful such that he ends up having a position to share in the inheritance of the children.

If you are a wise worker, that serves faithfully, you are not only a blessing to your employer, but you are positioned to share in the family's wealth tomorrow. I know of a family that needed some help with house chores when their kids were young. This helper was so faithful, dedicated and good cultured that if you were a visitor, you would not know he was only a helper in the house. After sometime they decided to send the boy to school while he was still serving in the house. He grew up with the kids, went to college, later studied for a master's degree, he was given necessary referrals to get a good job, got married and went ahead to raise his own family. These kids are all grown up now, and he gathers together with them, each one with their own family, at large family functions. His views are now sought when important decisions are to be made about the extended family.

In other instances, you find people employed as Janitors in a company serve so faithfully that they end up becoming shareholders and members of the board of directors of the company later. Your faithful service today brings refreshing to your employer and is a seed for your great future.

Day 76   Be a Faithful Friend

A talebearer revealeth secrets: but he that is of a
faithful spirit concealeth the matter. Proverbs 11:13

Can secrets be trusted into your hands, can your friend trust
you? If you would be a faithful friend our society will be
better; if you would be a faithful spouse our society will be
better; if you would be faithful to God, our society will be
better.

A faithful servant or friend will keep secretes. Employees will
keep business secretes; they will conceal secretes of their boss.
That means, they would be trustworthy, they would be loyal. If
you are in the business world, in the market place, you don't
want to reveal your employer's secretes to his opponent; you
want to be committed to your boss. You don't want to keep his
secrete and use it for your personal gain either; No, you don't
want to do that.

May God find you faithful! 'He that is faithful will bring
refreshing'. May you be a source of refreshing too many
people today; and as you do that, the Bible says 'the faithful
one will abound with plenty'. May the Lord prosper your day,
in Jesus name, amen.

Day 77   Desist from Pride

> *"Only by pride cometh contention: but with the well advised is wisdom"* Proverbs 13:10

Pride, if allowed in your heart is not wisdom. Many disputes and quarrels can be avoided if we resist pride. Pride has a lot to do with an elevation of personal ego. A man will never act in pride if he is wise.

Look at this scripture in other version of the bible and it will bless you.

Pride is a spirit that manifests in our attitudes. It tends to exaggerate your gifting and capabilities. You feel insulted because of pride. You feel insulted because you think you are worth more than what people present you to be. Pride kills, and before it kills you, you must determine to kill it in your life. It states clearly in our devotional scripture today that we should desist from pride.

Proverbs 14:3 says *'In the mouth of a fool is a rod of pride, but the lips of the wise will preserve them'*. It is only a foolish person that will speak with pride in his mouth. One thing we know is that pride is a thing of the heart. Check your heart and run away from pride; ask God to help you, and it will be well with, in Jesus name. May God bless your day, amen.

Day 78   Pride Leads to Shame

> *"When pride comes, then comes shame: But with the humble is wisdom" Proverbs 11:2 NKJV*

I like the Good News Version of this scripture *'people who are proud will soon be disgraced; it is wiser to be modest'*. Why not maintain an attitude that will sustain you and keep you standing firm. Since pride is a thing of the heart, you need to examine yourself and admit it to your own self if you are proud. Pride will debase you if you don't deal with it on time. So you have to cry to God today, and He will help you.

The word 'humble' is also referred to as 'lowly'. Lowly means; you don't overrate yourself. Don't speak falsely out of pride; don't describe what you do not have. Don't overestimate your gifting – yes you are gifted, yes you have influence, but don't overestimate it. Rather, even present the facts in lowliness of heart. The Bible says, God resists the proud but he lifts up the lowly. I am asking you today specifically to ask the Lord to help you because pride leads to shame.

Lord I pray that you will grant us grace to live with lowliness of heart, and bless your people today, in Jesus name, amen.

Day 79   Pride Brings Down a Man

'Pride goes before destruction, and a haughty spirit before a fall' Proverbs 16:18 NKJV

Pride precedes destruction! The moment you notice pride in someone; watch out, he or she is on the way down if care is not taken. Pride will bring down a man! The bigger a man's ego is the greater the fall will be.

The earlier you can identify this problem in you, the quicker you would present yourself to God for help and therefore prevent the catastrophic danger that goes with pride, the better for you. Do not allow what you have or possess go to your head. It leads to arrogance and this result in a great fall.

Proverbs 16:5 says *'everyone that is proud in heart is an abomination to God'*. Notice that pride is a thing of the heart. Nobody else may know it but you. You need to search your heart today and determine to desist from pride. Pr. 15:25 says *'The Lord will destroy the house of the proud: but he will establish the border of the widow'*. This is an interesting verse – usually a widow is assumed to be helpless. However, this scripture makes it clear that a widow has God's help, while a proud man experiences God's wrath! Pr. 29:23 says *'a man's pride shall bring him low: but honour shall uphold the humble in spirit'*.

Think through because this may be what has delayed your promotion till date; this might be the reason why your spouse has been having problems with you. It could even be the reason why those who should have helped you seems to run away from you! I pray you will be wise and deal with any trace of pride in you, and may God bless you in Jesus name, amen.

Day 80   Pride Is Abomination

'Everyone that is proud in heart is an abomination to the Lord: though hand join in hand, he shall not be unpunished'. Proverbs 16:5

The subject of pride is very important and it is very difficult to teach. This is primarily because as this verse clearly states; it is a 'thing of the heart'. More so, there is both positive and negative dimension to it. You are the only one that can determine if you are proud in the negative sense of it – although people might detect it through your behaviours.

The proud offends God by self-exaltation; offends other people by self-preoccupation and bring themselves problems with self-declaration. The delusion increases until one fancies oneself so high as to be invulnerable (Oba. 3). Hear what God says in Obadiah 4 to the proud in heart, *'Though you ascend as high as the eagle, and though you set your nest among the stars, from there I will bring you down, says the Lord'.*

The Bible describes pride as an abomination to the Lord! Abomination is: 'anything that offends the spiritual, religious, or moral sense of a person and causes extreme disgust, hatred, or loathing'. It is something which is morally disgusting. It is in the same category with the worship of idols (Deut 7:25-26; 17:2-5); sexual transgression (Lev 18); practice of magic, witchcraft, and engaging in occult activities (Deut 18:9-14). Most of the Hebrew words translated "abomination" has the meaning of "impure," "filthy," and "unclean"- that which is foul-smelling and objectionable to a holy God.

Day 81   Be Careful With the Poor

'Rob not the poor, because he is poor: neither oppress the afflicted in the gate: For the Lord will plead their cause, and spoil the soul of those that spoil them'. Proverbs 22:22-23

When the bible talks about 'the gate' – it is a description of the place or position where the elders and the people of authority and power meet. Someone might be described to be powerful either because of position, wealth, prestige or share popularity. 'The gate' is also relative – it could be within a community, within a company or a defined group of people.

Whatever the arena in which you might have power, today's wisdom warns us to be careful how we deal with the poor in our sphere of influence. A poor person may be someone who is helpless in some way, or who does not readily have anyone to help them out in their situation. A poor person may be at your mercy employment-wise or accommodation-wise or someone in financial lack.

The word of wisdom today states that we should be careful how we deal with this category of people. When any action is taken that indicate that one is taking undue advantage over someone else that can be described as being poor, God is saying He will personally plead their cause and spoil the soul of those that spoil them! The Common English Bible version says in verse 23, *'The Lord will take their case and press life out of those who oppress them'*. So think twice before you deal wrongly with the poor, otherwise, you will be an opponent of God in the same 'boxing ring' – that would be very disastrous! As you face today, let the wisdom of wisdom dwell richly in your heart. God bless you.

Day 82   Help the Poor

*'Whoso stoppeth his ears at the cry of the poor, he
also shall cry himself, but shall not be heard'.
Proverbs 21:13*

In yesterday's devotion we learnt that we should not cheat or
mistreat the poor. Today, God is telling us to go a step further.
You might not have cheated nor mistreated the poor, but you
probably have closed your ears to the poor, you have not gone
the extra mile to help them.

The cry of any poor person in need of some kind of help might
not be an audible sound, but if we would notice they have need
and we respond, God would be happy with it. When we notice
the need or the lack, and we ignore their needy situation, we
have simply 'stopped' our ears at their cry. If we do this, God
says when we cry ourselves, we will not be heard!

What does God expect us to do? He expects us to go out of our
way as much as we have the capacity, to attend to any need we
can notice with the poor. We should go out of our ways to visit
the orphanage, the widow, the old age home, etc., and provide
the help they need. If we find people who need a job, or an
accommodation, etc., we should go out of our way to render
the help we are capable of rendering to them. When you do
this, when you are in need, even before you cry out, your voice
will be heard on high and help will gravitate towards you.
Today, you will prosper, great will be your peace, and may you
find help when you need it, in Jesus name. Amen.

Day 83   Sure Foundation for a Good Heritage

'Good people will have wealth to leave to their grandchildren, but the wealth of sinners will go to the righteous' Proverbs 13:22 GNT

The way to prepare for the future of your children and their own children is to lay a good foundation for them. This can be done in many ways. First, by being good, faithful and loyal in serving others today, you sow a good seed that your children will reap from in future. Secondly, living a godly life as an example to your children lays a solid foundation for their future. Consider today's scripture in amplified version; *'a good man leaves an inheritance (or moral stability and goodness) to his children's children, and the wealth of the sinner (finds its way eventually) into the hands of the righteous, for whom it was laid up'*.

It is a godly desire to work hard and gather great wealth to leave for your offspring. You however need to be determined to live a godly life, and to invest time and energy in raising your children in a godly way. The way to secure the future of the wealth of your children is to gather your wealth legally, live a godly life in front of them, and to raise them godly.

My prayer for you as a father (or mother) or as one hoping to become one in future, is that you will prosper, and you will find joy in raising your children, and that you will find joy in your later days when you see your children and their own children living a godly life, and enjoying the wealth you have laid up for them, and also seeing them growing their own wealth in a godly manner, and enjoying it. May you find joy in your latter days, in Jesus name.

Day 84   Train up Your Children

*'Train up a child in the way he should go: and
when he is old, he will not depart from it'. Proverbs
22:6 NKJV*

As a parent, you have responsibility to be faithful both to God
and your children in the way you raise them. Faithfulness is
being loyal, being consistent and being able to use the gifts you
have in the way the giver of the gift has stipulated; being
committed. If you are not committed to the raising and training
of your children, you are not being faithful to God, neither are
you faithful to those children.

Do not let your business take you away from the responsibility
of raising your children well. The Good News version of
today's scripture says *'Teach children how they should live,
and they will remember it all their life'*. The greatest blessing
you can give to your children is to invest in their future by
training them. Not just giving them school fees to go to school;
but sit with them and point them in the right direction. Teach
them how to live their lives. Teach them the way to raise funds,
how to spend money, how to be clean, how to speak the truth,
how to read the word of God, how to serve God, how to be
good in the society; teach them the culture of working hard,
how to raise and live in a happy family. If you don't do this,
you will be regarded as an unfaithful parent.

Train your children; and when you see them in future, you sure
will be glad you did. And God will certainly be happy with
you. The assurance of a great tomorrow for your kids depend
on what you do today!

Day 85   Kids Are Prone to Foolishness!

'Foolishness is bound in the heart of a child; but the rod of correction shall drive it far from him'
Proverbs 22:15

Our scripture today points us to a striking truth that many do not realise, or are not willing to accept. If you are a child, sorry, this is the truth - you are faced with the challenge of frequently being tempted to behave foolishly. As a parent, face the fact – this is what we have in our hands to deal with! Let's look at the Message version 'young people are prone to foolishness and fads; the cure comes through tough minded discipline'.

It is a natural thing for young people to think and act in ways that are not right. The Bible states that the cure for this foolishness is through tough minded discipline. It will be unfaithfulness to God and to the child if you don't commit yourself to see to it that you assist your children to overcome this challenge. If we neglect to correct them, probably because of societal issues, it will be the greatest injustice we will be guilty of against the next generation. The future of that child will be jeopardised. Be involved in the life of your kids and be determined, not only to point them to the right direction to go in life, but also to discipline them when they go in the wrong way.

If you discipline your children when necessary, you will guide the child in the way of truth and understanding. As long as you do it in love, you would have proved to that child that the future is being sustained. If you are a child right now, be glad if your parents are giving you appropriate discipline; it is a sign that you are loved. Remember Pr. 3:12, *'because the Lord disciplines those he loves, as a father the son he delights in'* *(NIV).*

Day 86   Don't Hesitate to Discipline Children

> *Withhold not correction from the child: for if thou beatest him with the rod, he shall not die. Thou shall beat him with the rod, and shall deliver his soul from hell' Proverbs 23:13-14*

As the children grow, they begin to understand things better, and they will be glad that they were raised well.

Good News Bible says, *'Don't hesitate to discipline children. A good spanking won't kill them. As a matter of fact, it may save their lives'*. Many a times you want to show that you are a loving parent – and most fathers are loving, same with most mothers. But the Bible is saying don't hesitate to discipline them. If you would spank them in love, it would do more good than if you spare the rod, and spoil the child. Our society is in crisis today because there are too many spoiled children roaming around!

There are several youths who are wishing that when they were much younger they were given closer attention and corrected when they were taking the wrong steps. Many of my older friends who were raised in this society through appropriate discipline and are now of good character acknowledge the fact that it helped them to build who they are today. Unfortunately, these same people that are currently parents are shying away from appropriate discipline for their children because of current misguided societal values. Let's give this a thought and repent.

Have you been faithful to God and your children in this regard? Hesitating to discipline children does not equate to love; rather, a good spanking will not kill them – quite the opposite in fact. May God give you understanding, in Jesus name, amen.

Day 87   Be Slow to Get Angry

'If you stay calm you are wise, but if you have a hot temper, you only show how stupid you are'
Proverbs 14:29 GNB

Today we will start the discussion about managing and preventing the spread of anger in the community. Our scripture for today's devotional is an interesting one – look at it again in the Message version 'slowness to anger make for deep understanding; a quick-tempered person stockpiles stupidity'.

To be slow to get angry is referred to here as a sign of wisdom and understanding, while being quick tempered shows stupidity! Maintaining your calmness when you have been offended is certainly a difficult thing – but we need to make up our minds to give adequate consideration to today's scripture, it says we can control our emotions.

Let's choose to do that – be slow to be angry. Give a lot of thought to your situation before you talk or take any action. Some people refer to the fact that they would rather express their anger and not be like a hypocrite, but I have found out that it is more difficult not to sin when we quickly respond in anger.

The key point here is; 'be slow to getting angry'. You will agree with me that we can prevent a lot of problem in the family, among friends, at work, or somewhere in the community, if only we will 'be slow to be angry'! As you face your day, remember this word of wisdom. God bless you.

Day 88   Answer Softly – It Is Wisdom

'A soft answer turneth away wrath: but grievous words stir up anger' Proverbs 15:1

Every day we are faced with the challenge of being tempted to be angry in our dealings with people. It is also important to note that what we say to people, or how we respond to others, can make others to be angry. The Message version says *'A gentle response defuses anger, but a sharp tongue kindles a temper-fire'*.

When communication begins between two people, each person's response and counter response will determine the direction and likely end of the conversation. On a general note, hot tempered response leads to sustained argument that can end up in a bad place. The believer can be trained to control how conversations go in the marketplace, or in the family. This is because we have the spirit of God in us and He can help us overcome the natural tendencies of the flesh. Eph. 4:26 (New Century Version) says *'When you are angry, do not sin, and be sure to stop being angry before the end of the day'* – we are not immune from anger, but we have the ability to stop being angry if we will respond to the promptings of the Holy Spirit.

As you face the day, determine not to be annoyed by what you hear and if you feel angry, be slow to respond and give a soft response. Be careful how you talk to people so that they do not get angry. Consider the following scriptures (New Century Version): Pr. 15:18 *'people with quick tempers cause trouble, but those who control their tempers stop quarrel'*; Pr. 15:28 *'good people think before they answer, but the wicked simply pour out evil'*. Determine to be an agent of peace at home, at work and in the society. God will give you wisdom. You are blessed.

Day 89   Be Patient - Control Your Temper

> *'It is better to be patient than powerful. It is better to win control over yourself than over the whole city' Proverbs 16:32 GNB*
>
> *'Patience is better than strength. Controlling your temper is better than capturing a city' Proverbs 16:32 NCV*

Patience will help you control your temper better. You might not want to be angry in many instances, but if you are not patient enough, you may end up acting in anger. If a powerful leader is patient, he will lead better. It is no good to us if you can win a whole city and can't control your emotions. A husband, a wife, a boss, etc., will do better if they can be patient. American Standard Version says *'He that is slow to anger is better that the mighty; and he that ruleth his spirit, than he that taketh a city'*.

When you exercise patience in your day to day dealings, you are able to turn issues over in your mind and you will see things clearer and will succeed in hearing the promptings of the Holy Spirit; this will guide you to do what is right in all situations. If husband and wife can be patient with each other, there will be greatness, peace and less cases of divorce.

You might be in the right about a matter, and have the power and tactic to fight back in time of conflict, but if you exercise some patience, you might see a better way to respond in every conflict. As you face the day, remember this word of wisdom, and the Lord will give you understanding, in Jesus name, amen.

Day 90   Why Not Ignore the Transgression

'The discretion of a man deferreth his anger; and it is his glory to pass over a transgression' Proverbs 19:11

Instead of managing emotions when angry, it might just be best to simply ignore the transgression. This might not feel good to your flesh, but you would be surprised how much progress would be made if you are able to do this. Look at the scripture in the Amplified version *'Good sense makes a man restrain his anger, and it is his glory to overlook a transgression or an offense'*. Pass it over, just ignore it – it is good sense to forgive and forget!

There are four things we can notice from this scripture:

1) You have the ability to let it go, no matter how it hurts;
2) If you are sensible, you can, and will control your temper;
3) It is a great virtue to forgive and forget; and
4) Be smart and control your tongue.

If each person takes note of these four points, it will be easy to manage and control anger and maintain peace at home, at work, and in the society. I pray for families that have disputes today, that husband and wife will be wise and control their tongue; I pray for business relationships that are about to split because of conflicts that they will be wise to control their temper; I also pray for broken hearted and hurting people in our communities that they will be healed and encouraged so that relationships can be rebuilt and future can be preserved; in Jesus name. God bless your day, amen.